West Texas
⇒ T A L E S ⇐

West Texas TALES

MIKE COX

Charleston London

THE
History
PRESS

Published by The History Press
Charleston, SC 29403
www.historypress.net

Copyright © 2011 by Mike Cox
All rights reserved

First published 2011

Manufactured in the United States

ISBN 978.1.60949.329.5

Library of Congress Cataloging-in-Publication Data
Cox, Mike, 1948-
West Texas tales / Mike Cox.
p. cm.
ISBN 978-1-60949-329-5
1. Texas, West--History--Anecdotes. 2. Texas, West--Social life and customs--Anecdotes.
3. Folklore--Texas, West. 4. Tales--Texas, West. 5. Texas, West--Biography--Anecdotes. I.
Title.
F386.6.C692 2011
976.4'9--dc22
2011014421

Contents

Acknowledgements 9

Introduction 11

INDIAN TROUBLES

If She Had to Die, Why Wait? 13

George Hazlewood Died Game 15

Reverend Dancer's Road 17

COWBOYS AND CATTLEMEN

Old Pecos 21

Range Wisdom 24

Barnhart: Once West Texas's Fort Worth 27

LAW AND DISORDER

Bad Nell Lived Up to Her Name 31

The Surly Stranger 33

John Pearl's Singular Distinction 36

Naughty Ole Santa 37

LOVE, TEXAS STYLE

Ladies Love Outlaws—Or Do They? 41

Leaping Lovers 43

CONTENTS

CHARACTERS

Judge Roy Bean's Doctor   47

The Hermit on the Hill   50

The Checker-Playin' Lawmaker   52

GONE AND MOSTLY FORGOTTEN

Eureka, Texas   55

Quito, Texas   58

Stiles, Texas   60

Sweetwater's Bluebonnet Hotel   63

HAINTS

The Ghost in Officers' Quarters No. 7   67

The McDow Water Hole   69

STRANGER THAN FICTION

The Civil War Almost Started in West Texas   73

The Devils River Wolf Girl   75

"Here's Your Murdered Man!"   77

Anomalous Artifacts: Stories Untold   79

CRITTERS

Old Three Toe   83

Camels across West Texas   85

Horses v. Cars   87

LAUGHING MATTERS

Whiskey's First Funeral   91

Wanna See a Badger Fight?   93

The General's Last Engagement   94

BLACK GOLD

The Real Story of Santa Rita No. 1   99

A Different Sort of Dry Hole   101

The Yates Hotel   103

Pansy Carpenter   106

CONTENTS

TREASURE TALES
Bill Nard's Lost Lead Mine   109
Joe Pruno's Gold   110

NECESSITIES
"When You Get Right Thirsty…"   113
Pass Them Biscuits, Please   115

WEATHER WONDERS
The Day the Catfish Froze   121
El Paso's Big Blow   124
Teacher Rode a Tornado   126

RIP
Did John Roan Carve His Own Tombstone?   129
Little Girl Grave   131
Body in the Bale   133

WHAT MAKES TEXAS…TEXAS
Pecan Games   137
Coffee in Merkel   138
Horse Troughs   141

RECOLLECTIONS
Hotblooded Over Ice   145
Loading Ammo for Buffalo Bill   149
The October Barrel   151

About the Author   155

Acknowledgements

A special thanks to my daughter Hallie Cox, who scanned most of the images used in this book. Much more technically savvy than her father, who began his writing career in the typewriter era, she also digitally "cleaned up" some of the images. I also want to express my appreciation for folks who graciously contributed photos: Palo Pinto County newspaper editor Mark Engerbretson; Erath County writer Sherri King; former Texas Department of Transportation colleague Dan Fulgham; old friend Roger T. Moore of Merkel, Texas; former Reagan County newspaper editor David Werst; Jerry Morgan, former owner of the *DeLeon Free Press*; and rancher-history buff C.B. Wilson of Dallas.

Introduction

A Prairie Home Companion's Garrison Keillor once opined in an eight-hundred-word essay that he considered eight-hundred-word essays just about the perfect form of writing. Telling a story or making a point in that number of words or less, he continued, could be compared with writing a sonnet. While most of the stories in this collection are not essays in the classical sense—and darn sure are not sonnets—each of them does just happen to be about eight hundred words long.

But the length of these fifty-one stories and the fact that they all have something to do with the history and folklore of West Texas is about all they have in common. Like a lonely mountain lion on the prowl, they cover a lot of territory, ranging from accounts of Indian depredations along the nineteenth-century Texas frontier to stories about ghost towns to the ongoing daily ritual of coffee-drinking gatherings where West Texans talk about everything from the weather to politics.

West Texas Tales is the first of a series of books I'll be writing that will focus on little-known stories I've picked up over the years. Each book will concentrate on one of Texas's diverse geographic regions. (But since I get to draw the imaginary boundaries for each of these areas, some overlapping will happen.) All that aside, it is no accident that I decided to start this series with West Texas, where my roots grow as deep as any water-sucking mesquite.

My grandmother (who figures in one of the tales in this book) was born in San Angelo in 1898, right in the middle of West Texas. That's where she grew up and in 1916 got married to my grandfather, a young newspaperman who had already started his own weekly newspaper in Big Lake but dreamed of working on a big city daily. He achieved that goal and then some. And though born near Austin in central Texas, Granddad spent some of his childhood in the West Texas town of Ballinger. My mother, born in Fort Worth ("Where the West Begins") in 1928, was one of their two daughters. She met her future husband in the fall of 1946 while both were newspaper reporters covering a sensational murder trial in Sweetwater, where by that time my grandfather worked as manager of the Sweetwater Chamber of Commerce.

In 1948, I came along. While I grew up in Austin, my first full-time newspaper job was as a reporter for the *San Angelo Standard-Times*. Covering the news in the afternoon and at night, during the day I nodded through classes at Angelo State University. From "Angelo," as locals shorten the name, I went to another West Texas newspaper, the *Lubbock Avalance-Journal*.

My first book, *Red Rooster Country* (Pioneer Publishers, 1970), was a collection of history and folklore originally published as feature stories in the San Angelo newspaper back when it reigned as the morning paper for a trade area in West Texas about the size of Ohio.

This book is a collection of tales originally published by newspapers subscribing to a weekly column I started in 2000 and continue to write, "Texas Tales." But the stories selected for inclusion in this anthology are not merely reprints. All of the fifty-plus pieces in *West Texas Tales* have been given a fresh edit, and many have been reworked or updated. Also, most of these tales are illustrated here for the first time.

To get back to Keillor and his notion of what constitutes the best form of storytelling, in declaring eight hundred words as the perfect length for a piece of writing, he wasn't saying that eight hundred words make a piece of writing perfect. That's impossible, but in putting together this book I've tried to select and arrange the best eight hundred words I could for each story.

Indian Troubles

IF SHE HAD TO DIE, WHY WAIT?

Unlike most states of the Union or those of the Confederacy, Texas fought two wars in the early 1860s.

One war, of course, was the South's bloody struggle against the North. Texas sent tens of thousands of men to fight for the Southern cause in a mass fratricide that left 600,000 people dead and ruined many more lives. The second war was primarily one of self-defense against hostile Indian tribes taking advantage of the absence of the U.S. military and the state's preoccupation with the larger war.

The Texas government tried to keep state troops, rangers or, at times, regular Confederate soldiers scouting the frontier of West Texas to ward off incursions. That effort provided some measure of safety, but for all practical purposes, Texas had to contract its frontier more than one hundred miles during the war.

Recently widowed, Elizabeth Russell Baker lived in Erath County on the bloody edge of settlement. One night during the war, the loud cries of owls near her cabin awakened her. She knew enough about the frontier to know that Comanches often imitated owls to communicate with one another at night. As she listened in growing terror, she could distinguish several different owls. Indeed, they seemed to be signaling one another. Clearly, Indians had encircled the log home she shared with her five children.

Mrs. Baker stayed in bed, listening to the periodic hooting, thinking the end of her life had come. Soon, she would join her late husband across the great divide. She hoped only that the end would be quick. But what of her children? She could hear their slow, steady breathing as they lay deep in sleep, oblivious to their pending fate. Perhaps, she prayed, the Comanches would spare them.

Having only a quilt for a door, she knew she stood no chance if the Indians decided to rush her cabin. She figured their hesitation came only in their uncertainty as to whether the cabin's occupants were few or many and whether they were armed. Probably the Comanches were stealthily counting horses in the pen, animals they would be stealing soon enough.

As she listened, trying to make her final peace, the owls seemed even closer to her cabin. It would be over in a few moments, she thought.

Then a sudden resolve swept over her. If she had to die that night, she saw no need to wait any longer. Throwing off her cover, Mrs. Baker jumped out of bed and went straight to the door in her nightgown. Jerking aside the quilt, she looked out into the moonlit night and yelled as loud as she could, "Come on and get me if you're gonna get me!"

Bracing for arrows in her chest, all she heard was the flapping of wings as a tree full of startled owls took flight.

Shortly before the war, roughly ninety miles southwest of where Mrs. Baker had her scare, real Indians nearly spoiled a wedding. On January 28, 1859, a preacher named William "Choctaw Bill" Robinson stood ready to unite a Coleman County couple in holy matrimony. But before he could ask the traditional question of whether anyone knew a reason why the couple should not be married, a raiding party of Comanches swooped down on the gathering and kidnapped the bride-to-be.

Friends of the groom and other men who did not kindly abide Indian depredations saddled up and pursued the young woman's captors. Finally catching up to the fleeing raiders, the men skirmished with the Indians and managed to recapture the lady who had been snatched from the altar. When the Coleman County posse returned with the bride, the wedding proceeded.

Not long after the Civil War, a family who lived in a cabin on Armstrong Creek in Erath County had just sat down for their evening meal when a lone Comanche Indian burst into their residence and wolfed down all their food. Baptist preacher R.D. Ross took the near-starving intruder to Dublin and insisted that people there treat him well. The Indian who had invited himself to supper stayed for a few days with the Bill Keith family. Once he had recovered sufficiently to travel, he managed to thank his benefactors and assure them no further Comanche raids would occur in the Dublin area.

Whether the grateful Indian had anything to do with it, or whether it was merely because the U.S. military and rangers were making progress keeping the frontier safe, no further attacks occurred in the Dublin area. Thereafter, folks took to calling Reverend Ross "Comanche Rube."

George Hazlewood Died Game

The flashlight beams crisscrossed in the darkness as the young men and women made their way through the post oak thicket.

Ernie May, who worked in the drugstore at Breckenridge's Burch Hotel, his wife and some of their friends were camping on Hubbard Creek off the old Canyon Road southwest of town. They had been fishing, but when the sun set, they built a campfire and had been sitting around it telling stories.

About midnight, their conversation drifted to the old days when hostile Indians prowled the wild country along the Clear Fork of the Brazos. That's when one of their number said he knew of some old graves not too far from their camp. Grabbing their flashlights, the campers followed their friend into the night. Not far from a landmark known as Rattlesnake Den, their guide's light illuminated three mounded graves topped with limestone slabs. Carved on one of the rocks they could see the word "Hazlewood" and the number "68."

While their guide had known where to find the graves, what happened next caught everyone by surprise. About thirty yards from the graves, Mrs. May walked up on an old rifle thrust barrel-first into the ground. Shining their lights on the rusty weapon, the adventuresome campers soon spotted a second old gun not far from the first.

When they later broke camp, May took the old rifles home with him. As word of the discovery spread, he agreed to loan them for display in the lobby of the National Theater. One of the weapons found near the graves was a flintlock rifle, and the other was described as "a Minnie ball caliber" rifle with a shortened barrel. The stocks had just about rotted off both weapons.

The discovery of the old guns soon made the weekly *Stephens County Sun*, which published a page-one story on April 28, 1933. "Old timers recall that Hazlewood was a great Indian fighter of many years agone," the newspaper said. "That he was trapped and killed by the red men but not before some of their own lives had been taken by this intrepid fighter."

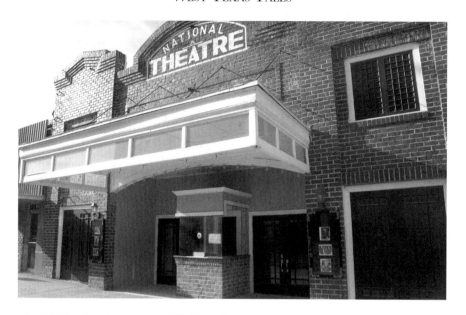

The old rifles found near George Hazlewood's grave went on display at the National Theater in Breckenridge. *Courtesy of Mark Engerbretson.*

Hazlewood, having died game, had won the respect of his attackers. "The Indians, as a mark of recognition to bravery, would leave an arrow sticking upright in the ground by a victim whose valor and fighting spirit they respected," the newspaper continued. "When Hazlewood's body was found, so goes the story, an arrow so upright bore evidence…to his courage."

Admitting that he had "picked up only a thread of facts," the author of the story said, "Mr. May would like to know and the *Sun* would like to publish" the rest of the story.

The *Sun* editor soon got more details from Elisha L. Christessen, then Stephens County's oldest resident. Christessen said one of the graves belonged to George Hazlewood, killed by Indians on March 2, 1868. Two of his daughters, Mrs. Donna Cain and Mrs. Belle Ferguson, still lived in San Angelo, he said.

"He was a good shot, a brave spirit and when caught out by a bunch of redskins he cut down on them and gave a mighty good account of himself," the old man said. "In fact, he killed three Indians and wounded very badly both a Negro and a Mexican who were along with the Indians." If it hadn't been for a strong south wind that blew sand into Hazlewood's eyes, he likely would have killed more of his attackers, Christessen said.

And then the old man offered some interesting insight on Indian fighting: Indians armed only with arrows and riding ponies almost always prevailed over any lone rider they encountered. The reason, Christessen said, was that the people caught out alone would quite understandably panic, spur their horse and ride the wind out of the animal in trying to escape.

On the other hand, he continued, Indians rode smarter, never winding their mounts if they could help it. Consequently, they usually could outlast a better mounted rider. Christessen said Indians also would fan out in their pursuit so that if the person they were after tried to turn one way or the other, he would ride into their line of fire.

Experienced fighters would high-tail it for cover. If they could manage to take a steep enough toll on their pursuers to demoralize the Indians, the warriors often would give up to cut their losses so they could fight another day.

Christessen said Hazelwood had been armed with a Sharp's rifle, a .50-caliber weapon that would kill a buffalo. It only fired one round at a time, but one account says some forty empty shells littered the ground around him when he was found. The Indians took that rifle, his horse and other equipment, but they left him unscalped as a testimony to his bully fight.

The Indians who killed Hazelwood rode up Hubbard Creek to its headwaters and raided a settler's house near the old Ledbetter salt walks in present Shackleford County. Soldiers from nearby Fort Griffin took up the trail and killed or captured the Indians.

Though several writers over the years have offered a version of the Hazelwood story, no one seems to have explained the old guns Mrs. May found that spring night sixty-five years after the battle. Nor has anything turned up indicating what happened to the vintage firearms beyond having been displayed for a time at a Breckenridge movie house.

REVEREND DANCER'S ROAD

Part of a formation known as the Riley Mountains, Dancer Peak rises about 600 feet above nearby State Highway 71 eight miles southeast of Llano. On a topographic map, the prominence is shown as being 1,714 feet above sea level. But the map does not tell the story behind the name.

Born in Tennessee on December 11, 1803, Jonas Franklin Dancer came to Texas with his wife and three children at some point in the 1840s. The 1850 U.S. Census shows him living in Travis County, running a mill on Bull Creek, a stream that fed into the Colorado River.

Around 1852, after a flood destroyed his mill, Dancer took his family to the northwest of Austin into what was then the far northern extent of Gillespie County. He settled on Honey Creek, a stream that began at the base of the peak that would one day bear his name. "The spot selected by Mr. Dancer was one of the most picturesque in the county," one nineteenth-century writer later observed. "Here game of all kinds and wild honey abounded in the greatest quantity."

Dancer trusted that the land had other gifts to give. Sustained by legends that Spaniards had once mined silver somewhere in the Hill Country, he believed that the rocky landscape concealed veins of silver and perhaps gold. Dancer spent several years prospecting in the area but never found any precious metals.

Though a seeker of nature's riches, as a Methodist preacher, he also believed in giving. As other settlers began to arrive, Dancer built the area's first church.

The preacher had chosen a fine place to settle, but it had one serious drawback. Being on the edge of settlement, that part of the state lay exposed to raids from hostile Indians, particularly the Comanches. Two years after homesteading on Honey Creek, Dancer added his name to a petition signed by 106 other area residents asking the governor to dispatch Texas Rangers to guard the area. Ranger companies did periodically go after the Indians, but not with enough regularity to do much good. Essentially, the settlers on the frontier were on their own.

In 1856, legislators carved a chunk of land from Gillespie County for a new county named Llano. Its heart lay only seventy-five miles from the capital city, but back then that distance amounted to a two- or three-day horseback ride, even longer in a wagon. The better the roads, of course, the easier the journey. With that in mind, in 1859 the more civic-minded men of Llano County took it upon themselves to build a road to Austin, probably the ancestor of present State Highway 29.

In the days before heavy equipment, road building involved moving big rocks, cutting brush and trees, burning out stumps and filling low spots and washes. Spreading gravel or building a roadbed and covering it with concrete or asphalt would not come until the twentieth century.

Dancer and other members of the community agreed to meet on May 23, 1859, to work on the Austin road. When Dancer arrived at the gathering place, no one else was there. He hobbled his horse and a packhorse, unloaded his tools, rolled up his sleeves and went to work.

"While thus engaged," chronicler Josiah Wilbarger later wrote in his classic book *Indian Depredations of Texas*, a party of Indians attacked Dancer.

Comanches terrorized early day West Texans. *Author's collection.*

"Being unarmed," Wilbarger continued, "Dancer fled to a deep ravine, closely pursued by the savages, who...attempted to rope him, but failed."

From a bluff overlooking the ravine, the Indians showered the preacher with arrows. "Finally overcome with loss of blood," Wilbarger went on, "he walked around in front of a projecting rock in the bluff, deliberately sat down on a rock bench and there expired."

A search party found Dancer's body the next day. But not until June 5 did newspaper readers in Austin learn of the preacher's violent demise. In that day's edition of the *Texas State Gazette*, editor John Marshall published a letter from Thomas Moore in Burnet: "Dear Sir—I send you a brief statement of the facts in regard to the killing of the Rev. Mr. Dancer, by the Indians about 25 miles S.W. of [Llano]...frequently preached here, and was quite an acceptable preacher in the Methodist church."

The same day Dancer died, Moore continued, a Mr. Gallagher "was shot and dangerously wounded by the Indians, though I learn he will probably recover. Mr. G lives in the same neighborhood where the Rev. Mr. Dancer was killed. About twenty-five Indians were seen by others the same day driving some 30 or 40 head of horses."

Moore concluded his letter to the newspaper with a familiar refrain: "How much longer must our bleeding frontier suffer these fiendish forays?"

In the case of the Comanches, it would be almost another twenty years. But it would be even longer before road building would become a function of government, not a task undertaken purely for community good by men like the Reverend Mr. Dancer, a literal Texas trailblazer.

Cowboys and Cattlemen

OLD PECOS

She didn't have a particularly feminine sounding name, but the old heifer they called Pecos sure came branded with a good story.

The tale came to light in the fall of 1928, when W.E. (Will) Pruett of Santa Rita, New Mexico, showed up in Alpine and Fort Davis looking for old acquaintances. His father, Philip H. Pruett, had been one of Fort Davis's earliest civilian settlers. He and his family had arrived at the small town adjacent to the frontier cavalry post in what is now Jeff Davis County in the summer of 1880.

Forty-eight years later, Will Pruett found only two people still living in Fort Davis who had been around during his youth, and only one person in Alpine. But at some point during his visit, he ran into a newspaper correspondent who interviewed him and wrote a story about him for the *Dallas Morning News*. (The journalist may have been Barry Scobee, who came to Fort Davis in 1917, but the piece does not have a byline.)

In 1876, Pruett related, his father took the family by train from White County in Arkansas to Trinidad, Colorado. From there, Philip Pruett carried his wife, Martha, and five kids (then eight-year-old Will was the oldest child) in a wagon to Santa Fe, New Mexico. That fall, Pruett bought a herd of forty shorthorn cattle and with his family and three cowboys left New Mexico for West Texas. All they had was one wagon and two horses. Along the way, they had to melt snow to provide drinking water for themselves and their stock.

With one wagon, two horses and forty head of short-horns, the Pruett family traveled five hundred miles from New Mexico to Ben Ficklin, Texas. *Author's collection.*

On New Year's Day 1877, they finally reached Ben Ficklin, at the time the seat of Tom Green County. The five-hundred-plus mile trip in the dead of winter had been hard on man and beast. "After our long and perilous journey," Pruett recalled, "all of our herd died of the Texas fever [a tick-borne illness] except four dogie calves and one 2-year-old heifer."

That sturdy heifer was Pecos, named after the river the Pruetts had to cross midway on their journey from Santa Fe to Texas. Not yet named, Pecos joined the herd about a week before Christmas. The Pruetts and their herders sat in camp on the north side of the river near the present town of Pecos when a rider approached. The man, who worked on a nearby farm, offered a two-year-old heifer to Pruett in exchange for a pound of coffee.

"Father told the Mexican that he had no saddle horse and that the heifer was wild and that he couldn't keep her with the bunch," Pruett remembered. The visitor said he would stay with them until the heifer settled down.

"So my father told him that he would give him the pound of coffee for the heifer," Pruett continued. "Then the Mexican went from the camp and in a little while came back with the heifer roped." The man tied her to a mesquite bush for the night. The next morning, they formally made the trade, cow for coffee. Soon after, presumably, the previous owner of the heifer enjoyed a hot cup of Joe on a cold December day.

Not long after acquiring Pecos, the Pruetts ran into a caravan of traders on their way to Mexico down the Chihuahua Trail. Their wagons were loaded

Courthouse in Ben Ficklin about the time the Pruetts hit town in 1877. *Author's collection.*

with dried buffalo meat. After that, Pruett said, they did not see anyone else for nineteen days straight, the time it took them to travel the stagecoach road from Horsehead Crossing on the Pecos to Ben Ficklin.

The Pruett family stayed in the Concho country until 1880, when the elder Pruett decided to relocate to Fort Davis. They pushed a herd of longhorns into that high country, according to Will Pruett, "the first bunch of stock cattle ever driven west of the Pecos." (That's not correct, but Pruett would not have known that.)

They lived two miles up Limpia Canyon, initially making a living by selling milk and butter to the military garrison. Later the family moved to Musquiz Canyon, where Pruett continued to run cattle. The pioneer rancher also played a role in setting up one of the area's first schools and helped blaze the road from Fort Davis to the new railroad town of Murphyville, later renamed Alpine.

Pruett kept Pecos, the heifer he got for a pound of coffee, for the rest of her long life. He had made a sharp trade. According to Will Pruett, Pecos lived for twenty-three years, giving birth to nineteen heifers and one steer calf.

"Her increase ran to more than 200 head in a few years," Pruett said in his 1928 interview. "One thousand dollars profit on the pound of coffee is a very conservative estimate of what the initial investment brought."

RANGE WISDOM

Before barbed wire crisscrossed Texas, the general roundup was a fundamental part of the cattle business. Every fall during the free range days, cattlemen pooled their resources and rode out to gather their stock. Cowboys checked each steer's brand, cutting out each head that belonged to his outfit. After that, ranchers either drove their cattle farther south for the winter or shipped them to market.

One of the biggest spreads in West Texas was owned by the Concho Cattle Company. The ranch covered major chunks of Concho, Runnels and Coleman Counties. The history of the ranch is well told in a master's thesis completed in 1939 by Irene Henderson, a graduate student at what was then Southwest Texas State Teacher's College in San Marcos, now Texas State University. Unlike most graduate research efforts, Henderson managed to work a lively story or two into her thesis. In large measure, that came from her interviews with one of the principals of the ranch, John Franklin Henderson (1864–1945)—her father.

One of the stories Henderson told his daughter concerned an early day instance of what now would be termed forced arbitration. The tale centers on Bob Price, another of the Concho Cattle Company principals. By all accounts, Price was a heck of a cattleman, a boss who proved a fair hand at playing Solomon.

Price was in charge of ten to fifteen cowboys out looking for cattle along the Concho River "this side of San Angelo," as Henderson related. While his men rounded up cattle, Price rode up on two cowboys locked in a heated argument over a steer with a poorly burned brand. Most of the time, a poor brand was the result of a botched job during spring branding. Sometimes, however, a hard-to-read brand meant some hide burner had altered the original brand to facilitate a clandestine change in ownership.

In this particular case, no one suspected an attempt at cattle thievery, but trouble was building like a thunderstorm on a hot, sticky afternoon. Neither cowboy could make out the brand on the steer's flank, but both cowboys claimed it for his owner.

The Texas cattle business revolved around the annual roundup. *Author's collection.*

Range boss Bob Price made a Solomon-like decision concerning a poorly branded steer. *Author's collection.*

Sometimes a brand could be successfully read by skinning off the hair over the mark with a sharp knife. Whether that had been tried or not, no one was backing down in his contention that the steer in question belonged to his boss. The only other way to determine ownership was to peel back the hide and read the brand in the tissue below. But that could only be done after the animal was dead—a conclusive but costly procedure.

Knowing that similar disputes had led to killings, Price feared that the situation was getting out of hand. Close as they were to blows or worse, the two wranglers at least had sense enough to ask Price, who had a reputation for fair dealing, to help settle the dispute.

"Whatever I do, you men will be satisfied?" Price asked.

Both said they would abide by his judgment.

At that, Price drew his six-shooter and put a .45 slug in the steer's head. With no other word, he wheeled his horse and rode off. Their ears ringing, the two wide-eyed cowboys had no further cause for argument. The only remaining issue was whether anyone wanted to cut some steaks or leave the carcass for the coyotes. But thanks to their boss's range wisdom, two hardheaded cowboys lived to ride another day.

BARNHART: ONCE WEST TEXAS'S FORT WORTH

Dust, bawling cattle, hell-raising cowboys and trains a half-mile long—that was Barnhart in the 1920s and '30s. Once a bustling if miniature version of Fort Worth, this unincorporated Irion County town is mighty quiet these days. The population in 2009 was only 169, and Barnhart's school closed in 1969. (If you want big-city life in these parts, go to the county seat of Mertzon, population 800-plus.)

Barnhart began when the Kansas City, Mexico and Orient Railroad cut through West Texas in 1911. The name honored William F. Barnhart, the land agent who obtained the right of way for the company's tracks west of San Angelo. Because of the Orient's location between major rail lines on the north and south, Barnhart quickly became an important shipping point for the vast chunk of real estate in between. Cattle and sheep poured out of West Texas on trains loaded at Barnhart. The town had everything the cowboys and railroaders needed: a hotel, cafés, a bank and a theater. A weekly newspaper, the *Barnhart Range*, provided the town with local news.

Given the remoteness of West Texas, old-fashioned trail drives continued to Barnhart long after their heyday elsewhere. In fact, all those cattle coming through began to cause local ranchers problems. To protect their pastures from over-grazing, ranchers started putting up more fences. That ended what may have been one of the last semi-free range holdouts in Texas.

To get around the problem, the Ozona-Barnhart Trap Co. was organized in 1924. A long, narrow swath of leased or purchased land stretching thirty-four miles from south of Ozona to Barnhart became Texas's last major cattle trail, a corridor one newspaper labeled "the world's most unusual highway." Along it, acreage for a series of six "traps" or pens—as important to cattle movement in those days as locks are to the Panama Canal—was acquired by the company and fenced to hold traveling livestock.

The company assessed five cents a head each night for cattle kept in one of the traps. Sheep, for one cent a head, could also be kept overnight in the traps. All a trail boss had to do was tell Ted Adkins, the company's Barnhart-based weigher, how many animals had stayed in a trap and pay him for that amount. No paperwork required. If a sheep shipper needed help getting his animals motivated to board a train, Adkins could furnish two lead goats—Lou and Whitney. Their follow-the-leader services cost fifty cents a carload.

Meanwhile, the railroad constructed large holding pens adjacent to its trackage at Barnhart. With ample infrastructure to serve a rancher's needs, sometimes as many as three trail drives a day hit town while trains with as many as seventy-five cattle cars hauled West Texas livestock to distant markets.

Cowboys like these worked all across West Texas in the 1880s. *Author's collection.*

Prosperity brought its problems. In April 1934, the town's former postmaster pled guilty in federal court to "conversion of funds." Barnhart, stuck pretty much out in the middle of nowhere, definitely lacked in the law and order department.

At some point in 1934, the town solicited assistance from the brother of one of the state's best-known peace officers, Texas Ranger captain Frank Hamer, to pacify its lawless element. That man was Harrison L. Hamer, a former ranger and just about as quick on the trigger as his older, more famous sibling. Frank Hamer had presided over the bloody demise of the outlaw couple Bonnie Parker and Clyde Barrow that May, but little brother Harrison had laid low a badman or two himself.

"Harrison is doing quite a bit of cleaning up in our town among the trash," wrote his sister Alicia Cumbie to their mother on August 20, 1934. "And they sure are getting hostile. This place sure needs someone to clean it up but he is sure up against a tough dirty bunch. He has a bunch of them in jail now."

The bad guys may have been "a tough dirty bunch," but Hamer, who apparently only stayed in Barnhart a short time before returning to his home in Del Rio, lived to old age and died of natural causes. Though what Hamer did in Barnhart seems to have generated practically no newspaper coverage, he evidently prevailed in restoring order.

Crime was not Barnhart's only problem in 1934. While that year the Associated Press declared Barnhart the busiest livestock shipping point in the nation, not every outbound train held jostling beeves. At the depth of the Depression, the federal government had begun buying cattle and having them shot to reduce supply, hoping to revive a market that had practically

Barnhart once rivaled Fort Worth in cattle shipping, but it's a near ghost town today. This old water tower was used by the railroad during the era of steam locomotives. *Photo by Mike Cox.*

dried up. Ranchers got paid on the number of cowhides they shipped out, and sheep skinners made good money turning their knives on dead cattle.

The Atchison, Topeka & Santa Fe eventually bought out the Orient, but Barnhart continued to flourish as a cow town through the 1940s. The advent of better roads and the widespread use of cattle trucks finally signaled an end to Barnhart's era as a major shipping center and twentieth-century Dodge City.

Law and Disorder

BAD NELL LIVED UP TO HER NAME

Wonder whatever happened to Bad Nell?

She was one of the scores of what euphemistically used to be called "tough women" (among other terms) who once hung out around Fort Griffin in its heyday as a cavalry post and buffalo hunter hide town. Nell might have slipped completely into the void of the historical unknown had it not been for an old man who showed up in the South Plains town of Tahoka back in 1932.

"Buckskin" Bowden, eighty-four, got a ride to Texas with a family of south-bound cotton pickers. Somehow a newspaper reporter got wind of him and did a story on the stooped, gray-breaded old-timer. Bowden said he first saw West Texas in 1878, as a nineteen-year-old runaway. Since then, he told a reporter who probably wasn't a third of his age, he had been to a lot of places but none as wild and wooly as old Fort Griffin. He was there from 1878 to 1880 and then moseyed on farther west to prospect for gold.

Fort Griffin and environs had no precious minerals, but as long as the army and buffalo hunters were around, there was enough money to attract professionals interested in obtaining some of it. That sort of crowd bred trouble, of course. "There were fights every night and killings were pretty common in spite of the soldiers being there," Bowden told the reporter. "The soldiers had to keep a heavy guard all the time to keep from getting their horses and supplies stolen. They were afraid to leave the fort except in groups of at least three or four."

The soldiers could not have been that shy about leaving the post, or else the saloon and brothel proprietors and employees would not have had any business. One of the ladies of the sporting crowd stood out in Bowden's memory more than a half century later. "Nell was an outlaw and a thief and a poker player, a good shot with a pistol and as good a horse rider as any man—and she played her game solitaire," Bowden said. "Otherwise she was a nice girl morally and had nothing to do with the hundred or more other tough women around the fort. I was her best friend, I guess, and just a casual acquaintance at that."

Bowden said Nell first arrived in the Fort Griffin country in 1876. She got a job on "Old Man

Bad Nell probably didn't look quite as attractive as the gambling gal depicted on this early postcard. *Author's collection.*

Ruins of the Fort Griffin sutler's store in 1935. *Author's collection.*

Johnson's" ranch, dressing as a man. She worked cattle all day and at night slept in a bunkhouse with four other cowboys who for six months did not know they had been sharing quarters with a young woman. By the time Bowden met her, she had turned from herding to hustling suckers at the gaming tables.

When Bowden and Nell showed up at a Christmas celebration at a saloon owned by a character called "Poker Jack," the owner threatened to reveal Nell's cross-dressing secret. She threatened to shoot him if he did, the old man recalled. Learning later that "Poker Jack" had indeed talked, Nell opted instead to beat him at his own game—gambling.

From Fort Griffin, Nell drifted north to Jacksboro, adjacent to Fort Richardson, and later to the Indian Territory with a husband she'd picked up along the way. A woman with the kind of plucky nature Nell obviously had probably lived a long life, but she does not show up in the indexes of any of the books written on Fort Griffin.

As for Bowden, he pulled out for Colorado and later prospected in Arizona. When the reporter talked to him in 1932, he was living in Colorado with the daughter of a former mining partner. He couldn't have lived much longer after that, but at least he got to tell the story of Bad Nell.

THE SURLY STRANGER

Whoever he was, he got a nice funeral.

Texas Ranger J.W. Fulgham and Reeves County deputy sheriff George Leakey left Pecos, Texas, for a ride down the Pecos River, looking for cattle thieves or fugitives in late August 1893. Back then, the Pecos was a good place to find either variety of criminal.

After an easy-paced thirteen-mile scout, the two lawmen camped for the night near Emigrant's Crossing, one of the river's two principal fords. The next morning, after coffee and breakfast, Fulgham and Leakey continued their trek southward along the snake-like river.

Not long after swinging into their saddles, the two officers noticed they were being followed at some distance by a solitary cowboy leading a packhorse. Wanting a closer look at the man, the men slowed their horses, assuming the rider would overtake them. But when they slowed, the cowboy behind them seemed to slow down, too.

Since the two officers didn't look much different from cowboys themselves, they were growing slightly suspicious at the man's apparent disdain of company. Reining their horses, the ranger and the deputy dismounted and

Texas Ranger J.W. Fulgham hated to kill the surly stranger, but he had no choice. *Courtesy of Dan Fulgham.*

waited for the stranger to catch up. When he did, he rode right by with not even so much as a "Howdy, gents," or a tug on his hat brim.

At that, the two officers got back on their horses and quickly caught up to the cowboy, one man on each side. Observing that the unfriendly horseman wore a pistol, Leakey identified himself as a deputy and asked the man if he was an officer. "I have been," he said, not elaborating.

Leakey shot a few more questions in his direction. "He answered all questions as to his name and destination in an abrupt and surly manner," the *Pecos News* reported a few days later. "His actions were those of a fugitive from justice."

The Reeves County deputy studied on the matter for a moment. "Jim," he told the ranger, "we will go to Pecos and take this man with us."

Hearing that, the stranger dropped the reins to his packhorse and reached for his pistol. The officers yelled for the rider to throw up his hands, but the cowboy raised his revolver instead. The ranger must have had his eyes fixed on the man's Colt, because his first bullet tore through the noncommunicative rider's gun hand. The smoke from that round blew back into Fulgham's eyes. Aiming by instinct, he pulled the trigger again, sending a slug into the stranger's chest and knocking him off his horse.

"By God, boys," the cowboy said, rising up on one arm. Then he slumped down, dead.

The officers left the body where it lay and rode to Pecos to summon Reeves County sheriff G.A. Frazier. The sheriff and Ranger Lon Oden accompanied the other two officers back to the scene, where Oden picked the dead cowboy's gun up and found it had been half cocked. Then they loaded the dead cowboy on a horse and took him to Pecos.

About all that the cowboy had to his name was a Colt revolver that had one black grip and one white, a memorandum book and a letter with the

Captain John R. Hughes after his retirement from the rangers. Hughes hired a lawyer who got Fulgham acquitted after only twelve minutes of jury deliberation. *Photo by L.A. Wilke.*

signature torn off. "Started to work for the flying E. Cow Co.," read one entry in his notebook. One sentence in the letter gave credence to the officers' belief that the cowboy was wanted by the law somewhere: "I would like to be back on the old creek, but you know I can't come."

The officers figured the man to be about twenty-three years old. The doctor who examined the body measured him at five feet, ten inches, guessed his weight at about 160 pounds and noted that he had gray eyes.

"Messrs. Fulgham and [Leakey] regret the occurrence very much," the Pecos newspaper account continued, "but from what we can learn from the facts of the case, we feel certain that they did nothing more than their duty required."

Unable to learn the man's identity, Sheriff Frazier saw to it that he got "a nice suit of clothes" and had him "buried in a quiet and genteel way, Rev. J.E. Sawders officiating."

By the end of the month, officers had the dead man tentatively identified. On August 31 in his monthly report to headquarters in Austin, Ranger Captain John R. Hughes offered the official version of the incident on the Pecos:

> *Private J.W. Fulgham in company with Deputy Sheriff George Leakey of Reeves County made scout down Pecos [R]iver in search of stolen horses. While out met a man armed with pistol. Attempted to arrest him for carrying pistol. He resisted and drew his pistol to shoot when Fulgham shot him twice killing him instantly. Have not found out who he is yet but suppose he is Charles Carroll. Out two days. Marched 50 miles.*

Back then, when a law enforcement officer killed someone in the line of duty, prosecutors tended to let a jury decide the matter even when the use of deadly force appeared justified. That's what happened in this case.

"Private J.W. Fulgham was tried at El Paso for killing Charles Carroll at Pecos in August," Hughes reported on November 4. "He was acquitted. The jury [was] only out 12 minutes. I employed J.M. Dean to defend him."

As for the surly Charles Carroll, if that's who he really was, about all that can be said of him was that he was foolhardy enough to pull a pistol on a ranger.

JOHN PEARL'S SINGULAR DISTINCTION

The old tintype, the only known image of John Pearl, hangs in a small frame on the wall in the Coleman County Museum. Considering why the picture is on display, this is altogether fitting. Pearl never got to know it, but he has the singular distinction of being the first and last man legally hanged in the county. (The number of cattle thieves caught in Coleman County who may have accidentally gotten tangled up in a rope suspended from a tree has not been reported.)

The jail in Coleman where Pearl spent time behind bars and later faced his execution was built in 1890 of limestone quarried from the nearby Santa Anna Mountains (not really mountains, but they are distinct landmarks). Contracted for on August 20, 1889, the new lockup set the county back nearly $16,000—$9,975 for the building and $5,600 for the all-important ironwork. The county dads accepted the turnkey job on April 26, 1890.

The lockup saw its share of miscreants and felons, but a decade passed before it held its first defendant in a capital case. Even then, the murder in question occurred in Brown County, not Coleman. The victim was Ed Tusker, a cotton farmer who had a place south of Bangs. In December 1900, he disappeared. When his friends and neighbors began to wonder where he had gone—no one had seen him since December 4—his hired hand said Tusker had decided to move back to his native Germany.

That hired hand was Pearl, who sold some of Tusker's cotton and cottonseed in Brownwood. He said Tusker had left him his wagon and team, along with other equipment and a bill of sale for some property. Tusker's friends and acquaintances, however, had heard nothing of any plans on his part to return to his native country. Within a week of his disappearance, people began searching for the farmer. Someone thought to check the stock tank on Tusker's place. On the second day of dragging operations, Tusker's body—weighted down with a large rock—was found.

Pearl was tried and convicted in Brown County. The jury's finding in regard to his punishment was easily written on a single piece of paper: death by hanging. But the defendant's defense attorneys argued for a change of venue and succeeded in getting their client a new trial, this time in Coleman County. District Attorney J.H. Baker, with J.O. Woodward in the second chair, prosecuted the case. Pearl's attorneys tried to save their client's life by proving he was insane, but the jury did not buy it. After hearing the prosecution's evidence, the jury found Pearl guilty and assessed his punishment as death.

Coleman County sheriff Bob Goodfellow, a Dallas native who had attended Baylor University, did not undertake his duty with any enthusiasm. But the law was the law, and he supervised the construction of a gallows inside the jail adjacent to the courthouse. Just as dutifully, he issued printed invitations to some fifty people to witness the event.

The sentence would be carried out on October 22, 1901. After allowing Pearl to speak for an hour and fifteen minutes to the two thousand or so citizens gathered outside the jail, Goodfellow reluctantly sprung the trap.

Dr. T.M. Hays of the nearby town of Santa Anna had been called on by the county to certify the condemned man's death. When he first put his stethoscope to the man's chest, the doctor recalled, "My heart was beating so hard that I couldn't be sure whether it was mine or his."

Even though he had no doubt that Pearl had been guilty as charged, his role in springing the trap bothered Goodfellow, who served as sheriff until November 6, 1906, for the rest of his life.

Naughty Ole Santa

Charles Dickens's *A Christmas Carol* stands as an enduring classic, but truth being stranger than fiction, Texas can claim one of the nation's more bizarre real-life holiday tales— the story of one particularly naughty Santa Claus.

On December 23, 1927, four gunmen—including one dressed as Santa Claus—robbed the First National Bank of Cisco. They escaped with $12,400, using two little girls for human shields as the town's police chief and another officer blazed away at them.

Downstate, Texas Ranger captain Tom Hickman sat in the Missouri, Kansas & Texas depot on Austin's Congress Avenue waiting for the afternoon "Katy" to Fort Worth. As the cowboy-turned-lawman cooled his boot heels, someone from the governor's office rushed up.

"Tom, the bank at Cisco has been robbed by a man dressed like Santa Claus," the messenger said. "He got away after a gunfight on the street. Get there as soon as you can."

Texas Ranger
Captain Tom
Hickman
coordinated
the search
for the Santa
Claus bank
robber. *Author's
collection.*

Reaching Cowtown, Hickman learned that his old friend Cisco police chief G.E. "Bit" Bedford had died of wounds suffered in the shootout with the robbers. Another Cisco officer, George Carmichael, had taken a bullet in the head, and doctors did not expect him to live. One of the robbers, Louis Davis, also lay mortally wounded. The other three gunmen, including a not-so-jolly bandit in a Santa Claus outfit, remained at large.

The ranger learned that Davis had been driven to Fort Worth in a hearse, a funeral home vehicle also used as an ambulance. A doctor had done all he could for Davis, essentially just dressing his wounds and shooting him up with painkiller. The robber would die, the only question being how soon. His removal to Fort Worth had not been to afford him better medical care but to save him from an agitated citizenry not inclined to let nature take its course.

Shoppers crowded a downtown ablaze with Christmas lights, but at the Tarrant County jail, Davis did not lie dying in a clean, well-lighted place. The infirmary smelled of disinfectant, but whatever commercial preparation the county used did a poor job of masking a permanent odor built up over the years by drunks and other law-breakers. A bare light bulb dangled above him on a long cord from the ceiling as Davis tossed in semi-consciousness on a bunk, covered with a thin blanket.

Hickman, an affable sort, tried to get Davis to name his accomplices and say where they might be hiding. But Davis, a down-on-his-luck family man with no criminal history, had run out of words and time.

Leaving the jail, Hickman noticed the hearse from Cisco parked across the street. The driver, trying to keep warm, had the motor running. The captain flashed his smile and his badge and asked for a ride to Cisco. At twenty miles an hour on an unpaved road, the trip would take four to five hours. Having had a long day, Hickman stretched out in the back to get some sleep.

Arriving in Cisco early on Christmas Eve, Hickman took over the search for the suspects, directing one of the largest manhunts the state had ever seen to that point in its history. His sergeant, Manuel T. "Lone Wolf" Gonzaullas, went up in an airplane as a spotter, participating in Texas's first-ever aerial search for criminals.

When lawmen jumped the three suspects near the Brazos River several days later, Ranger Cy Bradford wounded one, Marshall Ratliff, in a wild shootout. Bandits Robert Hill and Henry Helms managed to escape only to be taken into custody a few days later in nearby Graham. In eight days, the pair had made it only sixty-two miles from the bank they had robbed.

Of the three, Hill got a ninety-nine-year sentence for armed robbery and Helms eventually died in the electric chair for the murder of the two officers.

Ratliff, the man who had played Santa Claus with a pistol, also drew a death sentence for his role in the crime.

On November 19, 1929, annoyed at the slow pace of due process, a mob removed Ratliff from the county jail in Eastland and lynched him from a utility pole. The *Eastland Record-Telegram* covered the extra-judicial hanging thoroughly. The local citizenry clearly harbored no holiday spirit for the man who had donned a Santa Claus suit before sticking up their bank and killing two officers. The newspaper reported:

> *As souvenir hunters plucked at the body, a newspaperman met Clyde L. Garrett, Eastland county judge.*
>
> *"They've got Ratliff?" queried the judge.*
> *"Yes," the newspaperman answered.*
> *"I guess the county will have to bury him," the judge observed.*

As it turned out, Eastland County only had to pick up the tab for embalming the body. Ratliff's family saw to his burial.

Love, Texas Style

Ladies Love Outlaws—Or Do They?

Back in the 1870s, Texas Rangers had more than Bowie knives, six-shooters and lever-action Winchesters to choose from when it came to meting out justice on the frontier. Sometimes, passing a little information along to a reporter—in today's jargon that would be called "leaking" something—could serve the ends of justice quite well.

One example of rangers resorting to street justice traces to one day in early 1877 when a young man named Donaho took pen in hand to write a love letter to his sweetheart in Dallas. "Dear Darling," he began, off to an affectionate start. "'Tis with pleasure that I seat my self on the Banks of Llano River a Beautiful stream Rippling its way through the Western firmament and on each side…far as the eye Can behold is Mountains and prairies which vast herds of Buffalo roam…the lean Cyote Can be seen skulking around and all is lovely to the eye of one sad Boy."

Clearly, Donaho couldn't claim to be the world's best speller, and he apparently missed class the day they talked about capitalization, comma usage and run-on sentences, but as spring settled on Texas, he obviously had an eye for nature's beauty. He also had an eye for beautiful women, which was why he was "one sad Boy…" (Ellipses have been inserted to make his epistle easier to read.)

No less longingly than Romeo for Juliet, Donaho pined for his lovely Anna in faraway North Texas. "Could Anna But know the sad and shocking

A group of Texas Rangers about the time some of the lawmen found the outlaw's letter to his girlfriend and leaked it to the newspapers. *Author's collection.*

feelings that exist in my bosom," Donaho went on, "When I think of my Anna…Yes the Rose…the day star of my life I am winding my way through this barren Country to Mexico for my idea is to be a Western Warrior."

Did Donaho intend to join the cavalry or saddle up with the rangers? Obviously, he knew the days ahead would be dangerous. "We may never see each other again," he lamented, "but live with hope. My desire is that we shall both pass the short but treacherous hours away willing and well… Darling to dream of you by night and sigh for you by day."

Then, serenaded by the river, he really let it flow: "What a luxury for me it would be to behold your illustrious imige [image]…Yes Anna your eyes burn Liquid fire so flaming to my heart that [it] is irresistible."

Poor Donaho felt so lonely, so much longing for his darling Anna that he could hardly bear it. But the road before him seemingly stretched on and on. "As I travel along the Western horizon I seldom meet any one except the old hunter who is as grave as the Wind," he despaired in his awful solitude. "My only companion is three young men…we have a lonsime [lonesome] Time of it."

Finally, Donaho cut to the chase. He had not signed up as a "Western Warrior" to protect the frontier while wearing the blue uniform of a horse soldier or a ranger's white hat. In truth, Donaho rode the Owl Hoot Trail as an outlaw, having recently robbed the stagecoach between Austin and Fredericksburg. Now he skulked along the Llano, a man on the lam.

But like many young men, Donaho had hope for the future, a desire to make a good living at his chosen vocation and a comfortable home for the girl he wanted to marry. "We inhabit the Western Country and will Continue until we get Rich which I most emphatickly [emphatically] think we will and when we do I am Coming Back to dallas," he wrote. (Clearly, this was before the city earned its Big D status.)

"Wait for me Anna for I am solid with you…God is my witness I do love you…I am held to no Locality…Bound to no personal object except yourself… Yes wait for me and I will make you a jcncrous [generous] husband."

Alas, Anna never received the letter from her brazen beau. But she did learn of its contents when the *Galveston News* gleefully published it for all to enjoy after a Gillespie County ranging company captured Donaho and his fellow robbers. When the rangers went through his things, they found his unfinished love letter and cheerfully passed it on to the press.

The missive from the sad but bad Donaho caught the attention of readers in Texas and across the nation. Even the serious-minded *New York Times* considered Donaho's letter interesting enough to merit inclusion in its pages, publishing it on March 11, 1877.

The newspaper concluded: "The young man will have to serve five or ten years in the Penitentiary before he can lay his fortune at the feet of gentle Anna…and claim her hand."

Whether Anna waited for her love-struck swain to get out of the joint is not known, but having her relationship with an outlaw smeared all over the papers probably had a chilling effect on the romance.

LEAPING LOVERS

Knowing their love could never be, the young couple stood staring at the swirling river far below. One last kiss and then, holding hands, they leapt off the cliff, united forever in death—and legend.

Texas has at least four landmarks known as Lover's Leaps, and probably more. Telling the story of the Lover's Leap at Junction, in 1916 editor J.E. Grinstead fell back on verse in his magazine, *Grinstead's Graphic*: "Thus they stood a single moment, On that rocky, towering heap; Then, they named the place forever—As they made the Lover's Leap."

Postcard image of Junction's Lover's Leap. *Author's collection.*

The tales associated with precipices are touching, to be sure, but believing them takes a considerable leap of faith. Unrequited love has produced many a suicide, but jumping couples are far less common in fact than fiction. Even so, mankind has been enthralled by Lover's Leap stories for a long time.

Sappho of the Isle of Lesbos leaped into the Ionian Sea from a towering white rock because she had fallen in love with Phaon. In another ancient story, Hero, a young priestess of Apollo, hurled herself into the sea when she learned of her lover Leander's death. Marlowe transformed Hero's story into poetry in the sixteenth century.

The basic story crossed the Atlantic to North America and then slowly moved west with the development of the continent. Americans westernized the tale in an interesting way: instead of American girls and boys leaping from cliffs, most of the legends centered on the double suicide of Indians. Why Indians? Some scholars have suggested the preoccupation came from the American desire to romanticize the displaced noble red man. In other words, we will take your land but give you some enduring legends.

The best-known Lover's Leap in Texas is the cliff overlooking the Brazos River in Waco's Cameron Park. It's such a well-known landmark that there's a church named after it—Lover's Leap Baptist. (No, really. Check the Waco phone book.) As one early account summarized the story of this spot: "Here an Indian brave and his sweetheart jumped to their death because their parents would not let them marry."

One hundred miles south of Waco, Austin's Lover's Leap is Mount Bonnell. Austin being notable for doing things its own, weird way, the story here is backward. The woman who plunges to her doom from Mount Bonnell, a prominent feature above the Colorado River, is one Antonette, a European woman captured by the Comanches from the Spanish settlement of San Antonio. When her lover comes to rescue her from the Indians, they kill him. Seeing that, Antonette opts for death. The Austin story may be Texas's oldest example of a Lover's Leap legend. Newspaper writer and novelist James Burchett Ransom told the story for the first time in "Antonette's Leap and the Death of Legrand, or, A legend of the Colorado," in the *Austin Gazette* of March 18, 1840, when the capital city was not even a year old.

West Texas has two Lover's Leaps. One is the precipice two miles from Junction in Kimble County, first written about by Grinstead. The other is Texas's least-known Lover's Leap, a cliff on the Devils River. Again, the story here is a little different: an overly protective Indian chief and his warriors attacked the chief's daughter and her lover, both of them having fallen out of tribal favor. The smitten couple leaped to their death in the river just ahead of dad and his friends. The chief got to the bluff in time to see the lovesick couple sink beneath the water for the final time. At that, the chief called out that this must be the Devil's river and dropped dead, taken by a guilty conscience–induced heart attack. Of course, Indians of long ago did not practice Christianity and had no concept of hell. But all cultures understand a father's desire to protect his daughter, as well as the agony of love gone wrong.

Characters

Judge Roy Bean's Doctor

Even in the early 1900s, some doctors realized that smoking couldn't possbily be good for a person's health.

Trained at Hospital College of Medicine in Louisville, Kentucky, Dr. Donald T. Atkinson came to Texas in 1902 after graduation. He spent some time in Hopkins County and a brief interlude in Indian Territory (now Oklahoma) before establishing a practice at Del Rio.

One of his patients there was Sam Bean, son of the even-then famous Judge Roy Bean of Langtry, one of the Wild West's most singular characters. In his 1958 autobiography, *Texas Surgeon*, Atkinson told a story about Bean and his boy. The old judge, "beard lying thick upon his chest, at either hip a Colt .45," came to the doctor's office with son Sam. The younger Bean had been in Louisiana for a year. Now, back in drier West Texas, he was suffering daily chills, fever and sweats. He also had a cough. Weighing all the symptoms, the judge told Dr. Atkinson he thought his boy might have "consumption," the term for tuberculosis back then.

While the doctor continued his examination, the younger Bean asked if he could take a break to roll and smoke a cigarette. Atkinson asked Sam if he smoked a lot. "That boy of mine," the judge answered for his son, "smokes them coffin nails like a chimney. Only time he ain't smoking's when his face is filled with food."

The doctor reached a diagnosis: Sam Bean had chronic malaria, not TB. Atkinson gave the judge's son a prescription for the standard malaria

Judge Roy Bean holds forth at his famous Jersey Lilly Saloon in Langtry. *Author's collection.*

treatment of the day, a mixture of arsenic and quinine, and a little free advice—lay off the cigarettes.

The crusty judge, known for his impatience with cattle thieves and even miscreants, proceeded to lay down the law to his son about cigarettes. "Sam, y'hear? If I catch you with one in your mouth, I'll beat your brains out."

The young Bean saw the doctor several more times, and on each visit, he seemed to be doing a little better. But several months after his latest appointment, Sam took a sudden turn for the worse after getting into a fight with someone on a Del Rio street. Stabbed numerous times, he died of internal bleeding within two hours. Whether Sam had kicked his nicotine habit before then is not known.

Despite Judge Bean's tough-love approach to his son, the death of Sam must have hit the old man hard. But the loss of his boy did not dull his fealty to justice. The judge, in his official capacity as an elected justice of the peace, was out with two Val Verde County sheriff's deputies after cattle thieves when a severe norther blue in. None of the men had thought to bring coats. The deputies urged the judge to return to Langtry for warm clothes, but he would not hear of it. When sleet began to fall, the three men settled in for an uncomfortable night, warmed only by their sweaty saddle blankets.

The next morning, the judge was sick. His temperature shot up and he became delirious, babbling about his boyhood in Kentucky. The two deputies

Bean had no legal authority to hang a defendant, but that didn't stop the legend that he did. *Author's collection.*

slung Bean across a saddle and took him into town. Back in Langtry, they wired Del Rio for a doctor. The physician they requested was busy with another patient, so Atkinson was notified. He grabbed his bag and took the next westbound Southern Pacific train for Langtry.

When Atkinson got to the Jersey Lilly Saloon, he found the judge sitting at his desk. As Atkinson later recalled, "His hard old face was stained with a mulberry flush from fever. When he hawked and spat into his battered spittoon, I saw the saliva was rust-colored. The judge had pneumonia."

Atkinson did all he could for him, which was to give him a shot of codeine and some digitalis for his obviously weak heart. When Atkinson walked out of the room after having done all for Bean that he could, the judge had his head down on his desk. A few days later, the legendary Law West of the Pecos was dead.

Unfortunately for those who enjoy a good story, a literary autopsy of this tale reveals a preexisting condition that makes the real story anemic in comparison. Whether through faulty memory after the passage of more than a half century or a deliberate "stretching of the blanket" to enhance his story, the doctor's account of his medical relationship with the Beans must go into the chart as dead on arrival. While Atkinson's descriptions of the elder Bean and his demeanor have the ring of truth to them, at least based on what others have written about the crusty character, Roy Bean did not outlive his son.

The judge died on March 18, 1903. Sam Bean made it to May 7, 1907, more than four years later. Though Atkinson probably did treat the younger Bean for malaria, he hadn't moved to Del Rio until 1905, too late to have known the judge. More likely, the doctor injected what he had heard from others about Roy Bean into his story. Even so, an anti-smoking messsage published in 1958, six years before the U.S. surgeon general's first warning about cigarettes, shows the good doctor at least knew what he was talking about when it came to staying healthy.

THE HERMIT ON THE HILL

The late afternoon sun gold-plated the West Texas landscape, a fitting filter through which to view the deteriorating remnants of a hermit prospector's long-ago dream. Standing on a catclaw-and-greasewood covered hill, ranch owner C.B. Wilson and a guest surveyed a sprawling chunk of real estate that would be absolutely empty except for a few oil wells, a distant gas flare, a tank battery and two major east–west arteries—the nearby Union Pacific mainline and the adjacent Interstate 20 with its constant flow of eighteen-wheelers. Before the oil play began, this country lay even more desolate.

"Ward and Winkler counties are far out in the plains," the *San Antonio Light* said in late December 1921, "sparsely settled and seldom visited except by cowboys and hunters. Communication is slow and uncertain." So why would anyone want to live out their years in a dirt-floor dugout competing for shade with scorpions and rattlesnakes in the summer and warmed only by burning chopped railroad ties in the winter?

In a word, gold.

At some point after the Texas & Pacific Railroad laid track through what is now Ward County in 1881, most likely in the early 1900s, someone built a dugout on the northwest side of the railroad. They lived there for years, laboriously digging and blasting a long trench in an obsessive quest of gold ore. What's left of the dugout is about four miles east of Barstow on the Wilson Ranch. C.B. Wilson of Dallas, whose grandfather founded the multi-section spread in 1906, first heard about the hermit from his father. But the tale came with precious few details.

"All I know is that he was one-legged," Wilson says of the mysterious miner. "And when I first explored the dugout as a kid it was in a lot better shape than it is now."

By Wilson's guess, the dugout is fourteen by eighteen feet. Whoever built it did a good job. First, he blasted and dug a fairly square hole in the hard, rocky slant of ground deep enough to stand in. Then he piled flat rocks two or three layers high around the U-shaped excavation. On top of the rocks he laid old railroad crossties. He also used railroad ties and other pieces of lumber to build the front entrance, closing off the mouth of the U.

An old section of rail (much smaller than a modern piece of track) served as the dugout's ridgepole, with a cross-wise piece of pipe adding support. Upright crossties supported the rail ridgepole. The rafters were wooden, with long strips of tin or corrugated metal serving as the roof. On top of that, the builder piled dirt.

Whoever did all this work also sunk a square shaft through the rock as a chimney for his fireplace, which Wilson remembers having a rock-and-cement hearth when he first saw the dugout.

The roof has partially caved in, and sediment washed in by the occasional heavy rain has raised the floor level to the point a person can no longer stand upright in the shelter. Any trace of the prospector's mining operation disappeared in 2008 with the Union Pacific's construction of a two-mile siding adjacent to its main line.

All that's left of the mysterious hermit's well-built dugout. *Courtesy of C.B. Wilson.*

Wilson has no idea who the hermit was. "He must have died out here or gotten sick and went someplace else," he says. "I haven't found any old-timers who ever heard of him."

Lacking much fact, supposition will have to do. Since he had only one leg, the hermit could have been a former railroad worker. Back in the steam locomotive era, the railroad industry killed and maimed scores of workers every year. Or maybe the hermit was an old soldier living on a pension, possibly even a Civil War veteran. Quite possibly, he had mental health issues.

Whoever he was, he must have lived a Spartan lifestyle. He sure didn't leave much trash—a sardine can here, a coffee can there and a scattering of broken plates. "Back then, you could flag down a passing train," Wilson says. "He could have taken the T&P into Barstow or Pecos to buy whatever he needed."

Searching the area immediately around the dugout ruins, Wilson found three large Union Carbide can lids. The railroads used calcium carbide for their lanterns before batteries and generated electricity became the norm. The hermit might have scrounged remnants for his own lighting or used the one-hundred-pound capacity cans for storage.

Not long after the latest of the thirty or so freight trains that pass this spot daily rumbled by, a coyote dashed across the tracks seemingly headed straight toward the old dugout. He disappeared in the brush but soon walked into the open a hundred or so yards off and turned broadside, staring intently at where the hermit once lived. After watching Wilson and the visitor for a while, the animal moved back into the brush. But soon he reappeared, again scoping out the two humans. Clearly curious, the coyote slowly began to circle.

"If one thinks like a Native American," Wilson says, "you would say that coyote was a guardian spirit for our hermit and trying to figure out what we were doing in his house!"

With the sun and the temperature both beginning to drop, the two men headed back to Wilson's vehicle, leaving the mysterious hermit's old dugout to the coyotes and his fellow critters.

THE CHECKER-PLAYIN' LAWMAKER

Checkers has been a recreational fixture in Texas since before the Civil War. My grandmother taught me the game, and we had some spirited matches. Decades later, I instructed my daughter on checkers. At first, as my grandmother likely had done with me, I let Hallie win so she wouldn't get too discouraged. Proving a quick study, before long Hallie started allowing me a win every once in a while.

Obviously, it doesn't take long to learn about moves and jumps. Over the years, checkers has been referred to as "country chess" or "chess for the rest of us," but checkers is no less a thinking person's pursuit than that game of royals, bishops, knights, castles and pawns. Kings do figure in checkers, but players don't have to put up with a long cast of characters with varying powers.

Chess and checkers are both very old games. Some say the history of checkers dates to ancient Iraq, but most authorities agree that checkers (better known across most of the world as draughts) evolved from an Egyptian game called alquerque. (And no, that game is not where Albuquerque, New Mexico, got its name.) The French later started playing the game on a chess board and upped the number of pieces for each player to twelve, the beginning of checkers as played today.

Even though the game has been popular in America since the 1840s, no one seems to have compiled a list of famous Texas checker players. If anyone ever does, one name that should be included is W.R. "Bill" Chambers. Farmer and state representative from Brown County, Chambers liked the game so much that he used to play it by mail.

Born on April 10, 1880, in Alabama, Chambers came to Texas with his family as a teenager in 1893. They settled in Brown County near the Wolf Valley community. After attending Southwestern University in Georgetown, where he became quite adept at mathematics, Chambers returned to Brown County and spent twenty years as a schoolteacher in Wolf Valley and Lost Creek. That not being the most lucrative way to earn a living, he and his wife, Mary, also farmed.

Notes and Quotes from the Lives and Times of the Spencer Chambers Clan, a privately published family history compiled in 1986 by LaVerne Kilgore, says that the couple enjoyed a deserved reputation as community leaders and humanitarians. "The depression years were survived by growing and caning foods, and sharing what they had with friends and neighbors," the book notes. Playing checkers also must have helped during the hard times.

As the 1930s wound down, Chambers decided to try another kind of game. First elected to the House of Representatives in 1939, he served through 1947. Two years later, he won reelection and remained in office through the Fifty-fourth Legislature in 1957.

In the 1940s, the *Fort Worth Star-Telegram* spotlighted Chambers in an illustrated, cartoon-like feature called "Tip Top Texans: A Series of Sketches on Prominent Leaders." The item, which resembled a *Ripley's Believe it or*

Not cartoon, noted: "Checkers is his hobby—Having played the game with world famous players." Unfortunately for posterity, the newspaper piece did not name any of those world-famous players. It is known, however, that even as a youngster, Chambers played checkers by correspondence with relatives and friends by marking his moves on a penny postcard and waiting patiently for his opponent's mailed reply. To keep the postmaster and rural mail carrier out of the game, they used shorthand.

Checkers by correspondence is by the numbers. A checker board has thirty-two black squares, with each player starting with twelve black or red pieces. In postal play, the numbers 1 through 12, placed before a hyphen, represent the pieces, while the numbers 1 through 32 placed after a hyphen describe one of the squares. To make a move, a checkers-by-mail player might write "black 9-13," which means you move your black no. 9 piece to square no. 13. A jump or capture is written "black 15-22," meaning that the opponent who occupied square no. 18 is no more.

The game offers more than brain aerobics. Chambers would have appreciated an eight-point list, "Checkers and Life," developed by Waynesboro, Virginia minister and author Russell G. Waldrop:

1. The best players have experienced losses.
2. We…learn more from losing than…winning…
3. Everybody wants to be king.
4. Sometimes it's better to sacrifice…so…others can become king.
5. Kings make bigger targets.
6. We don't become kings all alone…
7. Jumping into and out of kingdom on one move may prove too dizzying for personal safety.
8. If you don't show up on time…you could lose the game.

Chambers kept playing checkers for most of the rest of his long life, which finally ended at the age of ninety on July 3, 1970. He's buried in the Wolf Valley Cemetery in Brown County.

Gone and Mostly Forgotten

Eureka, Texas

Newspapers these days get election results from official sources, but the process used to be a lot less formal. In the summer of 1891, for instance, the *San Angelo Standard* learned the outcome of the first election in Crockett County from two men who had just ridden in from Ozona. "W.S. Kelly and N.P. Lewis arrived from Crockett County yesterday and from them the *Standard* obtained the following approximately correct news of the election in that county," the West Texas newspaper reported.

Named for David Crockett, the county had existed on paper since 1875, first attached for judicial purposes to Kinney County and by 1885 to Val Verde County. Finally, on July 7, 1891, Crockett County's all-male electorate cast ballots for the first time. Residents voted in the county's first officeholders. But more important for posterity's sake, they picked the county seat.

As the *Standard* reported:

> *The vote for county seat with two boxes yet to hear from is as follows:*
> ** Joe Moss Ranch: Ozona 24, Eureka, 7.*
> ** Jackson Ranch: Ozona 9, Eureka, 3.*
> ** Henderson's Ranch: Ozona 12, Eureka, 6.*
> ** Couch's Ranch: Ozona 9, Eureka, 3.*

The Moore Ranch in 1890, shortly before Crockett County was being organized. *Author's collection.*

Doing the math showed fifty-four votes for Ozona to nineteen for Eureka. That, the *Standard* went on, "is so far above the two-third of all the votes that have already been counted that it is almost impossible for Eureka to get a one-third of the vote from the boxes not yet heard from, but we would not yet be certain that Ozona has won."

Of course, Ozona did become the county seat. Today, Eureka—first known as Couch Well—is not even a ghost town, only a ghost name.

A couple of weeks after the election, a correspondent known as "La Vaquero" (either someone who didn't know Spanish very well, a woman with a sense of humor or both) wrote a letter to the editor that the *Standard* published on August 11. Ozona, the local informant said, boomed with a capital B. "The town, although only a few weeks old, boasts of one store, with lumber on the ground for two more, one saloon, two restaurants, meat market, feed yard, boot shop, etc.," they wrote. "Most of the business is done in tents, although there are a dozen houses in course of construction and the sound of the saw and hammer is heard on every hand."

Despite the fact that the electorate had spoken on whether the capital of Crockett County should be the rapidly growing Ozona or Eureka, a judge in Val Verde County had a petition before him to overturn the results of the vote. "Although we have been informed that the…judge…has reversed his decision in regard to our county seat," the correspondent continued, "the people are paying no attention to it, as it is a settled fact that Ozona will still be the county seat, there being no opposite worth mentioning."

Indeed, the will of the people prevailed, no matter the validity of the election. "The land on which Ozona is situated is patented and belongs to E.M. Powell," the newspaper report continued. Powell had

> *generously donated to the town a good well, with 18-foot Eclipse windmill and cistern, also all lands for public buildings such as courthouse, jail, churches, etc.*
>
> *He has also just completed a nice school…24 x 50, which has also been donated to the town, his idea being to build a good town regardless of the cost to himself, as he has a large body of land in the county which will enhance in value as the town improves.*
>
> *Joe Moss, our handsome surveyor* [something of a clue that the letter writer was a cowgirl], *is his agent, and is kept constantly busy selling lots and showing prospectors around.*

So far, some seventy-five lots had been sold, the letter writer said. And though reports had made the rounds that the lots went for "enormous prices," the author strove to set the record straight: "Right here I wish to state that the size of the residence lots are 200 square and can be bought from $25 to $50, according to location, one-third cash, balance on time. Compared with the size of lots in other towns (50 x 100) they are cheaper than any town in the state."

In addition to the sale of lots, Moss and Powell were drilling two more wells in the new town, enough to ensure "abundance of pure water for all purposes."

"La Vaquero," though writing under an ambiguous name, had no doubt as to the future of Ozona and Crockett County. "Prospectors are coming in every day," the dispatch concluded, "and the majority of them invest before leaving, well satisfied that they have found the best portion of the stockman's paradise."

QUITO, TEXAS

The ghostliest of ghost towns are those that existed only on paper as blocks and lots on a grid of never-graded streets crisscrossing an unrealized dream. And surely one of the least known was Quito, Texas, not to be confused with the city of 1.5-plus million that is the capital of Ecuador.

Unlike Shafter, Thurber or scores of other Lone Star ghost towns, Quito has no picturesque ruins. It doesn't even have a bullet pock-marked historical marker. All that remains of Quito is a piece of paper filed away in the deed records of the Ward County clerk's office in Monahans and a scattering of purple glass fragments, china shards, rusty railroad spikes and other detritus left at two long-gone railroad stops.

W.P. Luce, Fort Worth entrepreneur and future oil man and Texas A&M University benefactor, filed a plat map of Quito Town on May 8, 1911. According to the document, unearthed by C.B. Wilson of Dallas, the town site would have been located in Section 143 along the Texas & Pacific Railroad, about five miles east of Barstow. The town plan showed fourteen named streets running north to south (Wagner, Church, Railroad, Plain, Dugas, Commerce, Main, Pecos, Roosevelt, Ward, Texas, Magnolia, Long and South) and the same amount of numbered streets from east to west.

Wilson, who owns the multi-section ranch that includes the land where Quito would have been, found the plat while looking for more documentation on his family's holdings. He hopes the map can be restored for posterity's sake, since it documents a town that never was.

Well, it sort of was. Quito and Quito Wells (also shown on railroad maps as Quito Water Station) were, respectively, a section house and water stop on the T&P when tracks came through that part of West Texas in 1881. As recently as the 1950s, Quito continued as a flag stop for both passenger trains and buses. But the railroad abandoned the facilities years ago, and no structures remain today.

In the early days, however, the railroad maintained points at regular intervals along its trackage for water stops (to accommodate steam-powered trains) and workers who handled track maintenance along their section, usually six miles of rail. By the T&P's reckoning, Quito Water Station lay

630.69 miles west of Texarkana, the point where the line entered Texas, and the Quito town site was 3.60 miles west of the wells.

So why would anyone want a town that then and even now is miles from anywhere? The answer is what could be found another 2.3 miles west of Quito—a quarry developed by the railroad to capitalize on an outcropping of Santa Rosa sandstone more popularly known as Pecos red sandstone. That long-abandoned quarry, once seventy feet deep but now partially filled with sediment from a rare torrential rain, produced stone that built courthouses and business buildings across the state. One of the better known of the surviving structures is the ornate Ellis County courthouse in Waxahachie.

On paper, Quito covered a full section, 640 acres, with some 6,000 lots. In examining the deed records, Wilson found that 325 people purchased lots between May 1911 and January 1915. Of those, 266 persons bought individual lots, with the others buying multiple lots. Harry D. Woodward of Denver, who if nothing else must have been an eternal optimist, bought 1,100 lots for $18,000—big money back then.

Wilson did not recognize any Pecos, Barstow or Pyote family names among the buyers, noting no sales to anyone from Ward or Reeves Counties. "It seems pretty clear that the sales were to faraway places and hyped on some level because the locals were not participating," Wilson said.

Based on other town site promotions Wilson has seen in old newspapers, Luce had salesmen operating on commission who did road shows touting

Texas & Pacific steam engines like this one stopped at Quito for water and occasionally for passengers. *Author's collection.*

the investment virtues of Quito. The farther from Ward County, the better the sales. W.F. McCool of Sedgwick County in Kansas bought sixty lots.

Prices ranged from a low of $5.50 a lot to $100.00 a lot. The quarry west of Quito soon ceased operations, and the planned town went nowhere. While Luce and his agents might have made some money on the deal, the various buyers did not. Eventually, Wilson's grandfather acquired the section and added it to his ranch holdings.

Why the railroad chose Quito as a place name remains a matter of speculation. Quito is Spanish for "remove," "take off," "take away" and other variants. Maybe someone came up with that name in relation to the quarry and the ongoing removal of sandstone from it. No matter, it's a fitting name for a development that saw a lot of people's money "quito-ed."

STILES, TEXAS

The old courthouse at Stiles is a monument to bad judgment. When lawmakers carved 1,130 sections from Tom Green County in 1903 to form a new county, a spot near Centralia Draw, not far from the Middle Concho River, was picked as the county seat. They named the place Stiles in honor of Gordon Stiles, one of the men who donated land for a town site. Soon a wooden courthouse went up.

Seven years later, the county had grown to the point where it needed a bigger, more permanent courthouse. The county commissioners hired a contractor from Comanche, and with limestone quarried not far away, a two-story courthouse soon rose up over the flat land. Completed in the fall of 1911, the new structure had barely been dedicated before bad judgment came into play. A local rancher refused to give up right of way for the approaching Orient Railroad. The railroad, shrugging its figurative shoulders, laid its tracks twenty miles to the southwest of Stiles. This route went past a rain-collecting depression in the well-baked West Texas landscape known as the Big Lake. A town named Big Lake developed nearby, but Stiles remained the county seat—for the time being.

Another major misjudgment associated with the courthouse came on February 19, 1918. On that day, Henry Japson, who had been sheriff and tax collector since the county was created, got in an argument with James Belcher, a friend of his. Succumbing to very poor judgment, the sheriff pulled his pistol and shot and killed Belcher. Then he walked down the hall to his office, shut the door and killed himself with the next bullet in the cylinder of his six-shooter.

Old Reagan County Courthouse at Stiles, Texas. *Courtesy of David Werst.*

The idea of being his own jury and executioner may have come to him from a case he had worked in 1907, someone else's misjudgment. A Stiles-area rancher killed another man who was sweet on his wife. The gunman telephoned Sheriff Japson and said, "There are two dead people out here and by the time you get here there'll be a third." When the man hung up, he killed himself.

By 1925, Big Lake and its railroad connection had become the commercial center of the county. The county set an election to determine whether Stiles should remain the county seat or whether the county offices should be moved to Big Lake. Big Lake won nearly two to one.

With no railroad and no county officials, Stiles steadily dropped in population. The old courthouse served as a community center and briefly as a school. As late as 1966, the county kept a road maintenance office on the first floor, but it eventually left and the place stood abandoned. By the 1990s, the one-time capitol of Reagan County stood dilapidated, though it still had a roof.

The culmination of the most recent misjudgment associated with the old courthouse's history came on Christmas Day 1999. On his third try, a thrill-

Fire started by an arsonist gutted the building. *Courtesy of David Werst.*

seeking arsonist succeeded in torching the structure. For his misjudgment, the man got a ten-year probated sentence.

David Werst, who along with his dad, Mike, used to run the *Big Lake Wildcat*, took color photographs of the burning building that day. "We were just sick," he recalled. "There were plans to restore the old courthouse."

The old stone walls still stand and possibly are strong enough to support rebuilding, but that would cost a lot more money. The county lost a large percentage of population in the last census, and rebuilding an old courthouse in the middle of nowhere is not likely to be a front-burner project anytime in the foreseeable future.

A state historical marker gives the barebones history of this barebones limestone building, but a more detailed marker explaining all the misjudgments that took place in it or around it would be more fitting.

Sweetwater's Bluebonnet Hotel

Now surrounded by so many two-hundred-foot-tall wind turbines that it has become the wind power capital of the nation, Sweetwater used to have a more traditional skyscraper—the seven-story Bluebonnet Hotel.

Back when U.S. Highway 80 ran through the heart of town, a 1937 vintage postcard labeled "Broadway of America, Sweetwater, Texas," shows the hotel dominating the view. The Bluebonnet was as familiar to Sweetwater residents as the University of Texas tower is to Austinites or the flying red horse atop the Magnolia Building in Dallas used to be for folks in Big D.

For years, the 120-room Bluebonnet enjoyed a reputation as a favorite stopping place for West Texas travelers. For someone in Dallas heading to the oil fields, the hotel made a logical overnight stopping place. Ditto for someone driving from Austin to Amarillo.

H.A. Allen, a Lampasas native who came to Sweetwater in 1921 and opened a car dealership, built the hotel in 1927. At the time, America still reveled in the pre-Depression prosperity and wild speculation of the 1920s. Even during the Depression, the Bluebonnet held its own, mainly because in those days a hotel was simply where you spent the night. The newfangled tourist courts, later known as motels, had a slightly seedy image. Outlaws like Bonnie and Clyde stayed in tourist courts. Respectable people spent the night in hotels. Sweetwater had been a

The Bluebonnet Hotel once dominated Sweetwater's skyline, but the Bluebonnet wilted. *Author's collection.*

railroad crossroads before automobile travel became common, and the Bluebonnet had accommodated many a railroad man over the years. Not to mention people connected with the oil industry, cattlemen—anyone needing a room for the night.

Beyond its role as a hostelry, the Bluebonnet reigned as the social center of Sweetwater and its trade area. The civic clubs met there each week, high schools and colleges held their sports banquets there, conventions used the hotel's meeting rooms.

During the economic boom that came with World War II, which for Sweetwater began with the opening of Avenger Field, the hotel enjoyed a flourishing business.

The Bluebonnet also saw some shady dealings. Not long after the army opened the new air base, the federal government brought conspiracy charges against two men for allegedly taking kickbacks during construction of the flying field. Testimony revealed that delivery of the illicit money—more than $6,000 when that was enough to buy a nice house—took place in a room at the Bluebonnet.

Starting in early 1943, the field began training female pilots. Most of them arrived by train and walked to the nearby Bluebonnet, where they spent their first night before reporting for duty at Avenger. Deanie Bishop Parish alighted from a passenger car at the Sweetwater depot from her native Avon Park, Florida. As soon as she got her luggage, she got a room at the Bluebonnet. "Several girls were there," Mrs. Parish recalled when interviewed by Dallas writer Bryan Woolley in 2005. "They told us there would be transportation the next day to take us out to [the field]. We were dressed in our finest dresses and our hats and our white gloves. We walked outside, and there stood three cattle trucks."

In 1944, a year before his death at sixty-six, Allen sold the Bluebonnet to a firm in Fort Worth. Another oil boom after the war kept its rooms mostly full, but in 1947, the hotel changed hands again.

As the stigma surrounding motels began to wane, and with the rise of automobile travel and the decline of train travel, high-rise hotels in city centers, particularly in smaller communities, began to lose business. In early 1960, California rancher-investor L.M. Mathisen bought the Sweetwater Hotel and renamed it in his honor. But by the end of the year, the hotel was in receivership and eventually acquired a new owner.

Despite everything, the hotel—back with its original name—remained open until the summer of 1967, its fortieth year of operation. On August 17 that year, a Thursday afternoon, black smoke began to pour from the top of the Nolan County landmark. Sweetwater firemen managed to save the building from complete destruction, but the top floor, a once-ornate ballroom, had been gutted. The rest of the old hotel had sustained heavy smoke and water damage. Some thirty guests had been registered that day, most of them oil company workers out in the field when the fire broke out. No one suffered any injuries.

Though the Bluebonnet had wilted, it lasted another three years, standing empty in the heart of town. Thick dust covered the inside despite boarded lower windows, and the frayed green awning above the sidewalks running on two sides of the hotel blew gently in the frequent wind.

Civic leaders hoped someone would buy the property and restore the Bluebonnet, but it never happened. By then, Interstate 20 had replaced Highway 80 and traversed well to the south of downtown, with plenty of new motels to accommodate travelers. Eventually, in lieu of unpaid taxes, the City of Sweetwater took ownership of the hotel.

In 1970, the First National Bank of Sweetwater purchased the Bluebonnet and adjacent property and had the hotel razed. Using part of the area for a new parking lot, the bank built a new facility on the rest of the property two years after tearing down the hotel.

Today, the Bluebonnet survives only in the memory of Sweetwater old-timers and on the once ubiquitous postcards sold in the hotel's drugstore.

Haints

The Ghost in Officers' Quarters No. 7

A small light flickered through a broken pane of glass in the dilapidated old officers' quarters at Fort Concho. Glancing at the light, the folks who occupied the adjacent officers' quarters bolted their doors and left a loaded gun in a convenient location—just in case.

Established in 1867 on the Concho River to protect Texas from hostile Indians, the fort had been abandoned since 1889. The old fort had become a residential area of San Angelo known as the Fort Addition by the early 1900s.

Grown men and women did not believe the popular legend that Officers' Quarters No. 7 had a resident ghost, yet the town's younger generation found the two-story structure terrifying. The adults merely agreed strange things seemed to happen inside the house.

Interviewed by a reporter in the 1930s about a year and a half before her death, Mrs. Mary E. Rogers, who claimed to be the first Anglo child born at the old fort, said "mysterious things happened in that old house (No. 7). They just couldn't keep it rented."

The limestone quarters was built in 1877. Colonel Benjamin Grierson, commander of the post at the time, wrote his wife saying the building contained a "double set of quarters for unmarried officers." After the fort's abandonment, as were many of the other buildings, No. 7 was used as a private residence and occasionally rented out.

Officers' Row at Fort Concho during its heyday as a frontier cavalry post. *Author's collection.*

The haunted house label got attached—apparently by children—following the discovery of a murdered man in the old building about 1895 or '96. At the time of the murder, the house sat abandoned. Someone found the body of a man inside, shot to death. After that day, rumor and legend spread faster than rigor mortis.

Mrs. Rogers, who remembered a lot about the old fort, said the man killed had made his living trapping coyotes, wolves and badgers. Apparently he had been killed in a dispute over trapping rights. One woman said the man believed to have committed the murder later was killed himself over a matter of grazing rights. "He ran his sheep all over the country," she said. "There wasn't much water at the time, so a land owner told him, 'Don't drive your sheep in my pasture.'" But just like a scene out of a western movie, the determined sheep owner pushed his stock across the other man's land anyway.

The landowner and a companion were riding in a wagon one day when they saw the sheep owner coming. The passenger gave the man a rifle and ran. The driver stayed on the wagon as the herder approached. The sheep owner and purported creator of the ghost in No. 7 ended up with a bullet between his eyes.

The old government building could attract spooky living characters as well as the more ethereal sort. Mrs. Rogers said that when she was a young girl living with her family at the fort, two men once approached her and asked if her mother might have a candle. She said she was sure her mother did, and the two asked her to bring them one. "I brought them a candle and they went down into basement of No. 7," she continued. "The people next door saw a light over there that night."

The next day, she related, lawmen from Brownwood showed up looking for a pair who had robbed a ranching family and made off with two of their best horses. The officers spotted two horses hitched up behind No. 7, arrested the two men inside and took them back to Brownwood to face charges.

As for Mrs. Rogers, she "liked to got ate up" by her mother for giving the two strangers a candle.

***

Postscript: Though Mrs. Rogers had said she was the first white child born at the fort, Suzanne Campbell, head of the West Texas Collection at Angelo State University, says a couple of other pioneers also asserted they were the first Anglo kids in Tom Green County.

No. 7 remained in private hands as rental property for a long time, but it is now part of the Fort Concho National Historic Landmark. These days, it houses the fort's library-archives and an office.

According to tour guide Michael Smith, the staff at Fort Concho has heard of No. 7's supposed haunting, but no one reports having any spooky encounters in the old building. Indeed, most of the ghost hunter attention at the old fort gets focused on Officers' Quarters No. 1, where Colonel Grierson's young daughter, Edith, died of typhoid fever on September 9, 1878. Many believe her ghost has stayed around after all these years.

The McDow Water Hole

A cold wind blowing in the dead of summer was the first clue something might be amiss at McDow water hole in Erath County. Then the folks living in the old cabin felt something touch their heads. Next they heard something scratching at the door. When they opened the door, a woman with babe in arms stood outside.

The water hole, about nine miles from Stephenville on Greene Creek, was named for Jim McDow, an early settler. McDow is barely connected to the ghost story that swirls around the landmark named in his honor, except that he was related to one Charlie Papworth.

Papworth, his wife Jenny and son Temple settled near the water hole in the spring of 1860, when Erath County lay on the edge of settled Texas.

The McDow Water Hole on Greene Creek still looks pretty, but something terribly ugly happened nearby. *Courtesy of Sherri Knight.*

The family lived in a stout log cabin, and Papworth made a modest living farming. Before long, Mrs. Papworth gave birth to a daughter.

Five years later, Papworth got word that his parents had died and that relatives were shipping all their possessions by rail to Texarkana. (At least that's the story. Texarkana did not have rail service until years later. More likely, the goods came by riverboat to Jefferson.) Wherever the freight went, he made arrangements with his neighbors and relatives, including McDow, to look after his family while he set out in his wagon to claim his inheritance. The trip took seven weeks.

When Papworth got back to Erath County, hard news awaited him. His wife and young daughter had disappeared. His seven-year-old son, who had been found hiding under a bed, was safe in the care of McDow and his family. McDow said he had gone to check on Mrs. Papworth and her children about three weeks before. He found the front door of their cabin open and the place deserted. Hearing the whimpering of a child, he discovered their son. All the boy could say was that his mother and sister had "left with a man." Other than their mysterious absence, no one could detect any signs of foul play.

Neither could anyone imagine what happened to Mrs. Papworth and her daughter. But one area resident, W.P. Brownlow, had a theory: Indians must have carried them off. He organized a posse to search for the pair, but he and the other riders returned empty handed.

Then someone remembered having seen this concerned citizen talking to Mrs. Papworth the afternoon before she went missing. When word of that got back to Papworth, he confronted Brownlow. The man denied knowing anything about the disappearance, though he did admit talking with Papworth's wife while he was gone.

Soon after his conversation with Papworth, Brownlow began spreading the rumor that Papworth had gone from farming to stealing livestock. Indeed, a considerable number of cattle and horses were being rustled in the area. Brownlow talked it up to the point that a local vigilance committee decided that no matter Papworth's bad luck in losing his wife and daughter, it was in the best interest of the community to string him up as a horse thief. The man who had last seen Papworth's wife was only too happy to lead the party that went to Papworth's cabin in the dead of night and took him to a large pecan tree not far away. They hanged Papworth, along with six other men supposedly involved in the thievery.

Luckily for Papworth, his son had managed to hide from the vigilantes. As soon as they rode off, leaving Papworth to strangle, the boy cut his father down. He was still alive, though the other six were not so lucky. The next day, Papworth bought a good horse and saddle and, with his son behind him, left Erath County for good.

Twenty years later, Brownlow made a deathbed confession that he had killed Jenny Papworth and her little girl, throwing their bodies into an abandoned well. Sometime later, the story goes, the bones of a woman and child were found when a flood washed out the old well.

Papworth never was heard of again, the killer was dead and the bones were buried. Then people started talking about seeing the ghostly visage of a woman and her little girl around the water hole.

The Papworth cabin is long gone, but the McDow water hole, the hanging tree and the story survive.

Stranger than Fiction

THE CIVIL WAR ALMOST STARTED IN WEST TEXAS

If the odds had been a bit more even on that March day in 1861, the first battle of the Civil War would have been at Fort Clark, Texas, not Fort Sumter, South Carolina.

The history books accurately report that the opening shot of the Civil War was fired on April 12, 1865, when Confederate artillery began shelling the brick-walled Federal coastal defense batteries in Charleston Harbor. But relations between the U.S. Army and forces supporting the South had been deteriorating well before that April morning in South Carolina.

In Texas, Federal troops occupied a string of frontier forts intended to protect travelers and settlers from hostile Indians. One of those posts was Fort Clark, established in 1852 on Las Moras Springs across from Brackettville (they just called it Brackett back then) in what is now Kinney County.

By March 1861, troops under Texas control, which is to say loyal to the South if not yet duly constituted Confederates, had gathered in Brackettville face to face with the Union garrison. As the officer in charge of the Texas soldiers negotiated with the commander of the fort for the surrender of the post, soldiers of one U.S. infantry company were less than enthusiastic about turning the fort over to a bunch of Rebels. Accordingly, they set fire to their quarters. Another infantry company trashed its quarters, smashing windows, doors, the inner walls of their barracks—even destroying iron bedsteads and burning their water barrels.

This is one of several cut stone buildings constructed at Fort Clark in 1857, four years before a potentially deadly Federal-Rebel faceoff took place at the post. *Author's collection.*

On the night of March 17, a group of soldiers left the fort and crossed the creek into Brackettville, where they tried to burn down a private residence, presumably the property of a Southern sympathizer. The soldiers also, in the more proper parlance of the day, "attempted to ravish (the) wife and daughter" of the owner.

That was more than enough reason for the Southerners to take on the Federal troops, but there were only eighteen of them against four companies. And most of those dozen and a half Texans had been a couple of miles from the fort when the Federal troops began destroying property. The rest of the ninety-six-member Texas outfit was scattered at various outposts and not available for immediate action. "If all of my company had been here there would have been a conflict," Texas captain Tervanion T. Teel reported a couple of days later.

Before open fighting broke out at the remote border post, the two sides finally agreed on a face-saving Federal surrender. The U.S. troops would fire their two artillery pieces as the Stars and Stripes came down from the post flagpole. Then they would march off and let the Texans take over.

The ceremony began as planned, but then the Federal officer in charge cheated. When they lowered the U.S. flag, the Federals cut the halliard and pulled the rope off the pulley in an attempt to keep the Southerners from hoisting the Texas flag over the fort.

"Upon reaching the flagstaff with my detachment," Teel reported to Austin, "I sent up four…men to the cross top and with a large rope, lowered the top mast, run the halliard through the pulley, hoisted it to its proper position, and run up our colors with a salute of the guns before the Federal Troops were out of sight."

A Texas "Fort Sumter" had narrowly been averted.

THE DEVILS RIVER WOLF GIRL

When the boy returned home that day he told his parents a story as horrifying as it was unbelievable. He had gone to San Felipe Springs, north of what is now Del Rio, to tend to his family's goat herd. He said he arrived in time to find a pack of wolves attacking the terrified stock. Among the wolves, he continued, ran a strange creature. Though loping on all fours like the other wolves, it appeared to be a naked girl.

The beautiful Devils River, flowing ninety-four miles from Sutton to Val Verde County, belongs to Texas. But the story of the Devils River wolf girl belongs to the world.

The tale had become part of border country folklore even before the river got its modern name in September 1848. That happened when former Texas Ranger captain Jack Hays and a party of men hoping to blaze a wagon road from San Antonio to El Paso rode up on the stream. Looking down on its glass-clear waters from a bluff in the middle of nowhere, Hays listened as his guide told him they had reached the San Pedro River.

"Saint Peter's, hell," Hays supposedly spat. "It looks like the devil's river to me."

Thirteen years earlier, in 1835, an Englishman named John Dent and his pregnant wife, Mollie Pertul Dent, came to the San Pedro–Devils River (somewhere along the way the apostrophe got dropped from "Devil's") and built a crude shelter. Originally from Georgia, the couple had come to that remote area so Dent could trap beaver along the Devils River north of present Del Rio. They camped near what would become Juno at a spot on the river he named Beaver Lake.

All went well until one night during a thunderstorm that May when Mollie went into labor. When it became evident that she was having problems, Dent saddled up to ride to the home of a Mexican goat herder to get help for his wife. No sooner had Dent explained the situation than a bolt of lightning struck and killed him. The goat herder and perhaps others rode to the couple's camp on the lake, only to find Mollie dead. She clearly had

The Devils River, shown here in this old postcard image, remains a wild and lonely West Texas stream. *Author's collection.*

managed to deliver her baby, but it was nowhere to be seen. Noting wolf tracks all around the campsite, the Mexicans concluded that a wolf had carried away and devoured the newborn.

A decade later, so the story goes, people in that part of Texas began to see a naked girl running with wolves. Though no one believed the boy who reported the first sighting, a couple of years later, a Mexican woman said she had seen two large wolves and a naked girl ripping into the carcass of a freshly killed goat. As she neared the creatures, she continued, they ran off. At first, the girl traveled on her hands and legs but eventually got up on her legs to keep up with the fleeing wolves.

Soon, others claimed to have seen the wolf girl. At some point (no dates go with this part of the story), a group of vaqueros rode out and managed to capture the wolf girl in a canyon. The vaqueros took her to a nearby ranch and offered her food, water and clothing—all of which she rejected. Locked in a room, she howled pitifully. Before long, other wolves answered her calls. And the howling kept getting closer and closer. Finally, a pack of wolves closed in on the ranch owner's corralled livestock. As the vaqueros shouted and shot to drive off the attacking lobos, the wolf girl broke from captivity and disappeared into the night with the other animals. The next morning, the vaqueros mounted up again in search of the wolf girl, but their effort proved fruitless. Her last reported sighting came in 1852.

Stories of humans raised by wolves go back a long time, all the way to the classic tale of Romulus and Remus. While that story had its origins in the days of the Roman Empire, the Indian subcontinent seems to be the locale for most wolf girl stories. One source says roughly one hundred wolf child stories have been reported in English, more in other languages. While the Devils River wolf girl legend is not unique from a worldwide perspective, it's one of Texas's most enduring folk tales.

"Here's Your Murdered Man!"

One of West Texas's more engaging mysteries began at Fort Griffin in 1877.

Near the Clear Fork of the Brazos on the western frontier of Texas, Fort Griffin was a U.S. cavalry post. The town that grew up next to it catered to the nonmilitary needs of the soldiers, was also a base for buffalo hunters and acquired a deserved reputation as one of the wild and woolliest towns in the West.

Ruins of Fort Griffin, where U.S. troops prevented James Brock from being lynched. *Author's collection.*

A smaller element of the population were the ranchers, folks who knew that once the Indians no longer posed a threat, a decent living could be made raising and selling cattle. James A. Brock and his two cousins, Frank and Ed Woosley, owned one of those early day West Texas ranches. Though the same blood flowed in their veins, it was well known in town that they disagreed over investments and other financial matters.

On May 22, 1877, Frank Woosley disappeared.

Local authorities, with the assistance of the military, organized search parties. Two hundred friendly Indians living in the area added in the manhunt. Brock offered a $1,000 reward for his missing family member.

When the search proved fruitless, suspicion began to focus on Brock. Woosley's family convinced local authorities that his cousin must have killed him in a step toward realizing sole ownership of the ranch and livestock. The criminal case against Brock, however, lacked two essential ingredients: the body of the victim or any other proof that a murder had occurred. Brock was released. Learning of that, the law-abiding citizenry decided to take the case to another court: Judge Lynch's. Only the intervention of federal troops saved Brock's neck from getting stretched.

Brock sold the ranch and left town, not to start a new life but to find his missing cousin. The people around Fort Griffin did not believe it, but Brock knew he had not killed his cousin.

In searching for Woosley, he spent all the money he made from the sale of the Fort Griffin property, borrowed and spent more and then took any kind of work he could get to fund his continuing search for the man whose disappearance had cost him his reputation and nearly his life. Nationwide, he circulated flyers offering a reward for information on his missing cousin.

The end came unexpectedly in a small Arkansas lumber town in 1891. A private detective, searching for someone else, noticed a man who fit Woosley's description. The detective contacted Brock, who immediately left for Arkansas.

Brock spotted his cousin at a train station in Augusta, Arkansas. "You scoundrel," he said, "I knew I'd catch you!"

The man at first denied his identity, but Brock's six-shooter refreshed his memory. His pistol tucked out of sight, Brock told Woosley that they were going back to Ohio so their family could see that he was not a murderer. At Memphis, Woosley tried to escape, but Brock got the drop on him and said if he attempted to get away again, he would kill him for real this time.

"Here's your murdered man!" Brock said in presenting Woosley to his astonished parents. Vindicated but no less bitter with the family that had accused him of murder, Brock turned and walked away. Returning to Texas, he settled in El Paso. He died there in 1912.

ANOMALOUS ARTIFACTS: STORIES UNTOLD

Archaeologists call cultural material found out of historical context "anomalous artifacts." But when ancient Chinese coins are dug up at an old frontier fort in West Texas, words like "mysterious" or "bizarre" seem more appropriate.

The coins from Asia turned up in Coke County at the site of Fort Chadbourne, a cavalry post established in October 1852 to help protect the frontier from hostile Indians. Five years later, the post became a stopping point on the Overland mail route. Soldiers stayed at the hilltop fort with its commanding view of the surrounding prairie until the beginning of the Civil War in 1861, after which Confederate forces occupied it. Federal troops returned for a short time in 1868, but the post was soon abandoned for good.

Less than a decade after the last soldiers marched off, Thomas and Lucinda Odom bought the abandoned fort as well as the property around it and founded a ranch that has been in the same family since then. Now owned by descendant Garland Richards and his wife, Lana, the fort is considered one of the most pristine military archaeological sites in the West. More than twenty thousand military artifacts, from buttons to weapons, have been found there over the years.

Among the thousands of artifacts are four well-worn Chinese coins, each with a square hole punched in its center. Two were minted during the Ching Dynasty, which began in 1644. One of the coins dates from 1736 to 1795 and the other from 1875 to 1908. Very interesting, but Texas isn't anywhere near Asia.

Though the discovery of the older coins could lead the more imaginative to conjure up the possibility of an unknown Chinese expedition to the New World, an archaeological report prepared by Richards and San Angelo avocational archaeologist Bill Yeates in 2005 concludes the coins "were probably brought [to Chadbourne] during the ranching period and had nothing to do with the time the fort was active." Not to mention not being remnants of a colonial-era visit by the Chinese.

Most likely, someone who passed through Fort Chadbourne carried the coins as a curiosity. Who knows? The Butterfield stage went to San Diego, California. Maybe someone got them there and, on his or her way back east, gave them to a kid who eventually lost them. Or maybe whoever had the coins knew they were valueless in the United States and simply threw them away. The possibilities go on and on.

Two early Spanish coins also are among the Fort Chadbourne artifact collection. Well-worn, they too probably were lost from someone's pocket or purse. Turns out that silver Spanish coins were legal tender in the United States until 1857.

A final set of anomalous artifacts found at the fort are six Republic of Texas–era military buttons. Soldiers of that area are not known to have been at the future site of the fort, but an early 1840s Indian-fighting expedition under Colonel John Henry Moore that traveled up the Colorado River could have stopped at the future site of Fort Chadbourne for water.

After Federal troops left the fort following Texas's secession from the Union, state militia and regular Confederate States of America soldiers occupied the fort at various times. Some of them may have been wearing uniforms with Republic of Texas surplus buttons.

A third possibility, which, based on a couple of letters found at the Center for American History in Austin, seems the most plausible in the opinion of Richards and Yeates, is that a character by the name of LeGrand Capers purchased the "Texas buttons," as he called them, for trade with the Indians. Capers, who is known to have spent some time at Chadbourne, traded with the Indians for skins and may have been a collector of Indian attire.

As Richards and Yeates conclude, "Every artifact has a story. None of them are really anomalous; we just do not know their story."

Critters

Old Three Toe

They called the killer Old Three Toe. Sometimes, he ate his victims while they were still alive. Occasionally, he seemed to kill purely for fun. Though roundly hated for what he did, most folks in Hall County grudgingly agreed he was plenty smart. In the early 1890s, when working hard from sunup to sunset earned a man a dollar a day, a $100 reward stood for anyone who could bring in the wily killer.

Three Toe did not prowl the South Plains out of meanness, for greed or revenge. He merely followed his instincts. Three Toe was a gray wolf. He killed livestock, not people.

Gray wolves once ranged all across Texas. An adult male could weigh up to 130 pounds. Standing three feet high, with a body stretching out to twice that length, these wolves could run faster than twenty miles an hour. Long before Europeans came to Texas, wolves preyed on buffalo, deer and pronghorn antelope, using their powerful jaws first to cripple and then to kill and eat. Sometimes the last two phases overlapped. By the mid- to late 1870s, with the great bison herd nearly gone, wolves quickly developed a taste for the cattle that followed.

"Reports from the ranges of West Texas indicate a large increase in the number of coyotes and lobo wolves," the *Eagle Pass Guide* reported in 1896, "and in the extent of their depredations on stock. It is not sheep and chickens that they now attack, but calves, colts and half-grown horned cattle. When a scalp bill is next presented to the Texas legislature there will be no division among the stockmen as to its merits."

Apparently, however, division on the issue did exist in the legislature. Lawmakers repealed the old bounty law and passed nothing to replace it. "Since the scalp law has been repealed," the same newspaper reported a few months later, "the stockmen...have found it necessary to form clubs for the extermination of wolves. Trappers are employed and each wolf killed costs the stockmen...about $3."

On the Edwards Plateau in West Texas, an estimated 150 wolves were caught just on one large ranch. "It pays to have them killed," the newspaper continued. "Forest Edwards said a few days ago that of his 7000 sheep he had lost nearly as many by the depredation of wolves as by disease, and that during the fall and winter the wolves had killed not less than 200 out of his flock."

Texans had never been reluctant to draw a bead on a wolf, but when the animals started killing cattle and sheep, ranchers began a war of extermination. Cowboys and herders shot them on sight. Hunters trailed them with dogs, set steel traps and lay out poisoned meat. Many wolves died, but they were a smart animal.

One wolf in Hall County had the reputation of being particularly wary. He had quickly associated the smell of man with the danger of sharp, cold steel. But every creature has the occasional bad day. Once, he missed the scent of danger and approached a cut of fresh meat. No one heard his scream when the steel jaws of the trap snapped on one of his legs, but a farmer found the trapped wolf the next morning. Before the farmer could raise his rifle, if indeed he had even been carrying one, the wolf tore its foot from the trap, leaving one toe and a piece of tendon behind. The close call added to the wolf's education and gave him his nickname, Old Three Toe. The distinctive track he left also demonstrated the impressive extent of his range and appetite.

One rancher in the area lost forty calves one spring. Old Three Toe's tracks could always be found in the vicinity. Soon, Old Three Toe had become the most wanted wolf on the Texas plains.

Instinct drove him to kill, and in the end, another powerful instinct led to his demise. A Hall County man happened to have his rifle with him when he encountered a pack of wolves fighting over a she-wolf. His guard down in the pursuit of romance, Old Three Toe caught a bullet. And another and another. Not until a slug slammed into his forehead did the big lobo go down for good.

Whether the man who finally settled accounts with Old Tree Toe collected the reward money went unreported, but he earned plenty of recognition in Hall County. The dead wolf went on display in Memphis with no less fanfare than the bullet-riddled body of a bank robber. Eventually, Old Three Toe's hide was shipped to a taxidermist, who preserved the snarling, trap-marked lobo for posterity. The mount stood for years in the town's First National Bank, an attention-getting reminder of the days when West Texas was wild in more ways than one.

CAMELS ACROSS WEST TEXAS

Funny how someone can get saddled with something another person ought to get the credit—or blame—for. Take Jefferson Davis, a West Point graduate from Mississippi who became president of the Confederate States of America. Just about everyone knows he led the South's unsuccessful attempt at separating itself from the rest of the Union. A lot of people also know that when Davis served as U.S. secretary of war in the mid-1850s, he experimented with using camels as a means of carrying supplies for the army. While true enough that as a cabinet member under President James Buchanan he signed off on what came to be called the Camel Experiment, it wasn't Davis's idea.

Colonel George H. Crossman, who first proposed giving camels a try as U.S. Army beasts of burden during the Seminole War in 1836, is the man who should get the credit for being the committee of one who invented the concept of using camels to carry men and freight in the American desert, including West Texas. Crossman was deputy quartermaster general when he had the idea, though it took nearly two decades to make it happen.

Like any good bureaucrat, Crossman tasked his assistant with looking into the matter further. Major Henry C. Wayne set out to learn everything he could about camels. He read up on them in Washington and consulted with the French minister, who had spent time in Persia and knew much about the beasts.

Satisfied that camels were indeed a good idea for the United States, Major Wayne forwarded to the secretary of war a report suggesting a camel program. He could make it happen, he said, for $30,000.

And he did. A shipment of thirty-three camels arrived at the Texas port of Indianola on May 13, 1856, and the army began using what one nineteenth-century writer referred to as "ships of the desert" in Texas, New Mexico and Arizona. The camels could travel up to fifty miles a day while carrying up

Early day drawing of U.S. sailors and the camels in their care. *Author's collection.*

to six hundred pounds of supplies and equipment. They didn't need much water and could ingest almost any plant, which is a lot more than could be said for horses or mules.

Initial experiments with the camels having shown promising results, the army brought forty-one more of the animals to Texas in 1857.

Though no one could deny that camels came particularly suited for operations in arid climes, few soldiers or teamsters felt highly of them. The animals required difficult-to-use harnesses and other tack. Packing camels proved a lot more difficult than loading up more traditional beasts of burden. On top of that, the unusual-looking and different-smelling beasts made the cavalry horses nervous. "The military officers found it hard to get any hostler to attend to the camels, towards which all the cavalrymen and troopers took a violent dislike," the *San Francisco Chronicle* reported in 1895 in an article reprinted in Texas.

Just as Crossman and Wayne's role in the army's unsuccessful camel experiment is not well known, a private sector attempt to put camels to good use in Texas never got much ink, either. A British ship carried two loads of camels to Galveston in 1858 for private use. After being offloaded, the animals were transported to the Watson Ranch, near Houston. While the camels earned their keep as pack animals, the ranch owner eventually gave up on the idea because they caused too much commotion when someone from the ranch took them into Houston.

From the camels' home base at Camp Verde in present Kerr County, the army mounted three expeditions across West Texas. The first, in 1857, went from Camp Verde to Fort Bliss at El Paso and eventually to Fort Tejon in California via (in Texas) San Antonio, Castroville, Fort Clark at Brackettville, Camp Hudson on the Devils River, Fort Stockton at Comanche Springs in present Reeves County and Fort Davis in present Jeff Davis County. Subsequent expeditions in 1859 and 1860 stayed in Texas, concentrating on the Big Bend area.

"In the last year or two of their stay at [military garrisons including Camp Verde] they were merely pensioners upon Uncle Sam's bounty, and were never brought into service," the *Chronicle* said of the camels thirty-five years after the final expedition.

The outbreak of the Civil War ended any military interest in camels. When Federal forces abandoned Texas, the camels stayed behind, left to fend for themselves. "The beasts were allowed to wander away at will," the San Francisco newspaper said. "They traveled in pairs, and sometimes in bunches of four and six, across the deserts and into the mountains…In some instances the camels multiplied, but in twenty years most of them died…or were killed by Indians."

However, some of the animals proved they could cling to life as tenaciously as their systems could conserve water. "Many a passenger on the Southern Pacific railroad trains has had a sight of some gaunt, bony and decrepit old camel away off in the distance," the newspaper article related.

Not until the 1890s, nearly four decades after their introduction to Texas and the Southwest, did the last of the camels finally disappear.

HORSES V. CARS

Until the internal combustion engine eventually made them obsolete as the primary mode of transportation, the horse amounted to the Texan's "automobile." With several generations of Texans now much more familiar with gas burners than oat-powered modes of locomotion, it is easy to think of horses and cars as virtually the same things. But the only similarity is that each, in their day, became the preferred means of personal transportation.

The portrayal of the horse in American popular culture, of course, has not led to an accurate general understanding of how those who lived in Texas in the eighteenth, nineteenth or early twentieth century got around. If you believe most western movies or remember the era of the black-and-white TV westerns, back in the day a horse stood instantly available and as untiring as any hunk of metal and plastic started with a key.

The truth is, as anyone who has read much about the West or spent any time shoveling out a corral can readily relate, a horse is an animal, not a machine. That said, horses require every bit as much maintenance as an automobile and are a whole lot less forgiving if their care gets short shrift.

Before automobiles, West Texans considered a horse indispensible. *Author's collection.*

One big difference between a horse and a car, of course, is mileage. A person can get behind the wheel of a car and, depending on how much gas they have in their tank and how strong or weak their own bladder is, can emerge three and a half hours later two hundred miles away. With a horse, back when it was the only alternative to walking, a good day's ride amounted to thirty miles. Experienced, determined riders on a good horse could push the distance factor to forty and even up to eighty miles. Riding a horse that hard, however, could leave it jaded or even permanently unfit for riding. Sometimes, an extremely tough ride could kill a horse.

To make it as easy on government stock as possible, the U.S. Army liked its cavalrymen to weigh 140 pounds or so. A bigger man was extra work for his mount, not to mention that he made an easier target for any enemy. The army way, when on the march, was for the men to be in the saddle forty-five minutes of every hour. For a quarter of each hour, the troops dismounted and walked ahead of their horses, giving their animals a chance to rest a bit and cool down. At noon, army horses on patrol would be unsaddled and allowed to graze and rest. That daily rythm led to the old cavalry expression of "forty miles a day on beans and hay."

Speaking of grazing, in fall or winter, anyone traveling by horseback had to carry horsefeed (oats, corn or hay) or depend on some place that had an available supply. In the spring, a hardy horse could get by on native grass, assuming it had not been spoiled to man-provided feed.

Those who prevailed in early Texas were those who learned how to best handle their horses. Generally, Texans could outride poorly trained and sometimes ill-mounted federal troops. Comanches, often described as having been the finest light cavalry in the world during their heyday, could sometimes outride either soldiers or Texans.

No matter how skilled the rider, a horse could not go faster than a gasoline-powered vehicle. But perception of speed is another thing. Texas storyteller J. Frank Dobie, who as a young man spent plenty of time in the saddle, had this to say about the difference: "Although machinery has reduced miles to minute decimals, it has not reduced the sense of speed felt by a horseman and shared by his horse. A running team of mustangs hitched to a buckboard will give the rider more sense of motion than the fastest automobile on a straight concrete road."

And a bag of feed costs a whole lot less than a tank of gas.

Laughing Matters

WHISKEY'S FIRST FUNERAL

They called him Whiskey for obvious reasons. A cowboy who worked on ranches along the Concho River in the top part of McCulloch County, Whiskey was known to take a drink or two or three. He won his nickname when he got so desperate for a drink one time that he traded his horse and saddle for a gallon of whiskey.

Whiskey cowboyed and drank back in the 1890s, long before Alcoholics Anonymous and the organization's twelve steps to sobriety. His friends probably didn't even know what the word "intervention" meant, but out of concern for their near-always sodden coworker and friend, they resolved to resort to a little tough love in the hope of at least tempering Whiskey's whiskey drinking.

Before relating the details of Whiskey's most sobering moment, it's important to understand the place and times. One of the principal communities of northern McCulloch County was Rochelle. The town offered all the necessities of life and, when the cemetery was started in 1894, at least one of the necessities of death. Rochelle did lack an undertaking establishment, but back then the burial process was not nearly as complicated as it would become. When someone died, his or her survivors took care of preparing the body and "laying it out" for visitation. A woman would cut and hem a shroud, while the menfolk built the dearly departed's coffin, using one by twelve planks and lining the box with white silk or satin. That

No images of the cowboy called "Whiskey" are known to exist, but this old snapshot shows the effect too much whiskey can have on a fellow's judgment. *Author's collection.*

amounted to a lot of work for a bereaved family, so the community took it as quite a sign of progress when the general store in Rochelle began stocking factory-made coffins. Some families, worried that sudden death might catch them short, bought a coffin and kept it in the barn until the need arose.

All this was of little concern to Whiskey, still young enough to believe that he would live forever. But when someone noticed him lying passed out in public, once again having drunk himself into a deep stupor, Whiskey's friends looked on it as an opportunity to have a little fun and perhaps teach their pal an important life lesson as well.

His cowboy pals scooped him up and carried his limp body to the general store. Next, they lowered him into one of the mass-produced coffins the store had in stock and folded his arms across his chest. Then, with a patience even the Grim Reaper would admire, they waited.

When Whiskey's eyes began fluttering as the alcohol started wearing off, the boys gathered around his coffin, doffed their Stetsons in mock respect and broke into a somber hymn. For a bewildering moment or so, Whiskey lay there thinking he must have been on the verge of being buried alive. He rose from the "dead" so scared that he vowed never to drink again. Of course, as his hangover settled in, he wished for a while that he had died.

As someone who knew the story later related, the incident touched Whiskey so deeply that he stayed sober for a whole week.

Whether Whiskey ever put the plug in the jug is not known today, but he long since got to be the guest of honor at a real funeral, whenever or wherever that was.

Wanna See a Badger Fight?

The cowpoke took a deep sip of lukewarm beer and then slid his mug down the bar for a refill. Casually glancing at the mirror behind the bar, he saw a young stranger walk into the saloon. His bloodshot eyes warmed, radiating pleasure and a glint of evil as he watched the neatly dressed drummer, a traveling salesman, gingerly approaching. Not only did the drummer appear to be a dandy, more than likely he hailed from that place Texans tended to dismiss as "Back East."

The cowboy sauntered over to the young gentleman.

"Buy you a drink, bud?"

"Well, I might take a glass of water."

"Hey, Joe," the cowboy yelled to the bartender, "this gentleman would like a glass of water."

As the drummer sipped his drink, the cowboy assessed the dude peddler.

"Listen friend, I see you're new in town. I bet you didn't even know we had a badger fight lined up today, did you?"

"Why no," he replied, wide-eyed, "I didn't. But what, sir, is a badger fight?"

"Well now, bud, you're in luck. I think you still might be in time to get in on this one. In fact, since you're new in town, we'll let you have the honors."

"The honors?"

"Yeah, com'on, I'll show you."

The cowboy stood up on a chair and announced: "Hey boys, this drummer's never seen a badger fight. I told him he was just in time for one today."

At that, the other boys grabbed their drinks and began moving upstairs. Quickly, the room above the saloon, used mostly for storage, was cleared to accommodate a crowd. Soon, a man came up the stairs hefting a big barrel. Another man came in with a ferocious-looking dog, straining on its leash.

A badger fight, someone explained to the drummer, was just that. The barrel held one of the stripe-faced mammals known for its vicious temper and sharp claws. As soon as the bets went down, the badger and the dog would fight to the death.

"To show this here drummer a good ole West Texas welcome," the lead cowboy announced, "we're gonna let him pull the badger outta the barrel."

The drummer couldn't believe his luck. After placing a chair atop a table, a couple of the cowboys carefully lifted the barrel and put it on the chair. With great ceremony, someone then ushered the drummer to a point near the barrel. "When you're ready," his new friend told the drummer, "reach up and pull that barrel down toward you. That old badger will come flying out right past you and lit straight into the dog."

Already composing in his mind the letter he would send his family to tell them of the singular honor he had been accorded, the proud drummer did as he had been told. Reaching up to put his hand on the top edge of the barrel, he jerked it as hard as he could.

As the cowboys roared in delight, weeks of accumulated slop flooded down on the hapless greenhorn.

Initiations like this happened all over the West. The modus operandi varied from perpetrator to perpetrator. Sometimes a full chamber pot (used as a "Porta Potty" before indoor plumbing) was inside the barrel instead of slop.

My grandfather, L.A. Wilke, who told me this story, says the good folks of Sonora were still laughing about this particular badger fight when he went there from San Angelo in 1915 to buy a printing press for a newspaper he was going to start publishing at Big Lake. Granddad would have only been eighteen at the time. Makes me wonder why the Sonora boys didn't try the stunt on him.

THE GENERAL'S LAST ENGAGEMENT

Anyone who knows anything about the history of World War II has heard of General Jonathan M. Wainwright. Far less known, however, is the story of

General Jonathan Wainwright, hero of Bataan, saw his last "action" in West Texas. *Library of Congress.*

his last skirmish, a brief engagement that occurred on a West Texas ranch in the late 1940s.

A soldier's son born at Fort Walla Walla in Washington State, the general did three separate tours of duty in Texas over a forty-year period that saw him rise in rank from second lieutenant to four-star general. He liked Texas so much that when he retired, he stayed, living out the rest of his life in San Antonio.

Freshly graduated from West Point in 1906, Lieutenant "Skinny" Wainwright got assigned to the First Cavalry and received orders for the distant and at that time peaceful Texas-Mexican border. Via Fort Sam Houston in San Antonio, Wainwright spent time at Fort Clark in Brackettville and later as the sole caretaker of recently deactivated Fort Duncan in Eagle Pass.

Wainwright left Texas in 1908 for the first in a succession of other posts, including combat in the Philippines, before returning to the Lone Star State in 1938 as brigadier general in command of the First Cavalry. He lived in the most imposing of the officers' quarters at Fort Clark, remaining there until new orders sent him once again to the Philippines in 1940.

Prior to Pearl Harbor, though Wainwright had been a crackerjack cavalry commander known for his tough-as-a-horseshoe spit and polish, he was just another officer and gentleman in a peacetime army. Oh, he also had a taste for whiskey, but so did most of the polo-playing horse soldiers who sat an officers' club bar stool as gracefully as a saddle.

But when he became the highest-ranking officer in the history of the U.S. Army to surrender a command, which is what happened after he realized he could no longer hold off a Japanese onslaught at Corregidor in 1942, his name became a household word. Surviving the infamous Bataan death march, he spent the rest of the war as a POW.

After the war, "Skinny" once again got orders for Texas as commander of the Fourth Army at Fort Sam. This time he arrived as a hero, having been awarded the Congressional Medal of Honor

Just a few months after his retirement in August 1947, the general and his longtime aide, Colonel O.I. Holman, left the Alamo City on a less-than-squad-level mission. Their objective was to harvest a couple of white-tail bucks on the Wheat Ranch in Sutton County. Holman's wife owned the ranch. The Wheat property adjoined a ranch about thirty miles southeast of Sonora owned by Jack Turney. In fact, anyone going to the Wheat Ranch had to drive through the Turney Ranch to get there.

Also heading toward the Turney Ranch that fall day were fourteen-year-old John Stokley and his cousin, Friess Turney. Friess's granddad owned the ranch. As the two teenagers drove along a two-rut road toward the Turney ranch headquarters, they spotted a beautiful, big-racked buck standing broadside to them on the side of a hill about 150 yards from their vehicle.

"We piled out with a .300 Savage and a .30-30 Model 94 Winchester and cut down on that deer," Stokley recalled. "After five or six rounds, it dawned on us that Jack Turney, who was a notorious practical joker, had put a fake deer up there. We walked up the hill and found it was just an old hide with a bunch of bullet holes in it attached to a big set of horns."

Indeed, the placing of a faux buck to attract the bullets of over-eager hunters may well be the prime prank among deer hunters, the hunting equivalent of surreptitiously cutting the barbs off your fishing buddy's hooks.

When the trigger-happy boys reached the ranch headquarters, everyone had a good laugh. Suddenly, one, two and then three distant rifle shots cracked the air. "After a dead silence for about a four-count, we heard another 'kapow,'" Stokley said.

A short time later, a late model car pulled up outside the ranch house where Stokley, his cousin and Jack Turney were still chuckling over Turney's joke. The Hero of Bataan and Holman emerged from the car to join in the laughter, apparently thinking they were laughing at the fact that Wainwright had been suckered in by the phony white-tail.

When Turney realized the general had also fallen for the fake buck, he started laughing even harder. "Hunters," Stokley summarized years later, "have creative imaginations." So, apparently, do old soldiers hankering for venison.

Black Gold

THE REAL STORY OF SANTA RITA NO. 1

The movie *The Rookie*, the story of a Big Lake High School baseball coach who makes it to the big leagues, begins with another story. A narrator explains how the oil field around Big Lake began with the Santa Rita No. 1, the discovery well on University of Texas–owned land in Reagan County that triggered the first West Texas oil boom and finally allowed UT to live up to its constitutional mandate of being a state univeristy "of the first class."

Early in director John Lee Hancock's 2002 film, viewers of *The Rookie* see two nuns walking in blowing dust in the middle of nowhere, scattering yellow rose petals. The sisters had invested in the drilling project and had been told by their priest to bless the site. The screenplay is based on a real story, Coach Jim Moore's, and so is this opening scene. But Hollywood, not surprisingly, took some license with the facts. This is the real story:

For $500, Frank T. Pickrell, a World War I veteran from El Paso, had optioned an oil lease on 436,360 acres of University of Texas land in four West Texas counties, one of them Reagan County. The option stipulated that he had to be drilling on the property within eighteen months. That, of course, would take some money. Pickrell's father-in-law put up $43,000, but Pickrell needed more. That's when he went shopping for investors, two of whom were Irish women from New York.

A skeptical priest told the women that if they intended to invest in an oil well sight unseen they had better seek the assistance of Santa Rita, the

Saint of the Impossible. When Pickrell left the Big Apple for Big Lake, the two Catholics—accounts don't say whether they really wore habits—gave Pickrell a sealed envelope filled with rose petals. The women asked that he climb to the top of the derrick and scatter the petals. Pickrell, happy to have the investors, promised he would.

Whether through divine intercession or simply good geological work, what happened next changed West Texas.

At 6:00 a.m. on May 28, 1923, Louella Cromwell, the wife of the driller, yelled for her husband Carl to come kill a rattlesnake by their front door. Cromwell got his shotgun and opened the door of their plank shack but found no rattlesnake. The hissing his wife had heard was gas escaping from the well, which was spewing oil sixty feet into the air.

"Oil was spilling all over the houses," Nora Locklin later recalled. (Her husband, Dee, worked for Cromwell for five dollars a day as a tool dresser.) "The white Leghorn chickens were soaked, the old milk cow jumped the fence and took off, [and] our garden was in a sad shape."

Cromwell and Locklin told their wives to stay put while they drove as fast as they could to Big Lake to buy some oil leases before word got out about the blowout. Both men succeeded in doing that, and they lived easy for a good while afterward.

The nearest pipeline being 125 miles away in Ranger, Pickrell needed some capital to be able to cash in on his new well. He sold sixteen sections of his lease to another company, with the provisio that they drill eight wells on the land. The first seven wells proved dry or low producers, but the eighth came in at 1,500 barrels a day. That marked the true beginning of production in the Permian Basin.

During the fifty-year anniversary celebration of the Santa Rita well in 1973, Reagan County rancher Billy Boyd remembered the hoopla attendant to the gusher. The Sunday after the well blew in, he said, a special train brought scores of people to the site from San Angelo. His family wanted to go see what all the fuss was about, but from his family's ranch five miles northwest of Stiles, the trip would be a long one. First they'd have to drive to Big Lake, then another fifteen miles west to the well site along a two-rut road. To save time, Mac Hartgrove decided to drive overland, a distance of only fifteen miles as the crow flew. The Boyds and the Frank Ingham family figured they'd follow in their cars, but they had two flat tires along the way and had to open ten ranch gates. The trip ended up taking four hours, longer than it would have the other way.

Meanwhile, the train from San Angelo had arrived at the new gusher. A vendor operating from a tent did a flourishing business selling cold sodas and

When Santa Rita No. 1 blew in, the West Texas oil boom began. This is how the well site looks today. *Photo by Mike Cox.*

hamburgers to the throng of visitors. But by the time the Boyds and the other family got there, the hamburgers were long gone and the ice had run out.

The oil from Santa Rita lasted a lot longer. With an original flow of one hundred barrels a day, a half century later the discovery well still made two to three barrels a day.

A Different Sort of Dry Hole

One of Texas's most impressive engineering feats is nothing but a hole in the ground today, an idea that tanked big time. In 1928, however, anything seemed possible, especially in West Texas. The newly discovered Hendricks field in Winkler County spouted five hundred barrels a day, and places like Pyote, Monahans and Wink became what one newspaper called "mushroom towns." The only thing rising faster than the available supply of crude was the price it fetched.

Unfortunately, the Roxana Petroleum Company (later Shell Oil) did not have a pipeline to get all that oil to a refinery. And hauling the crude to the nearest rail connection by truck over mostly unpaved roads would take a fleet of vehicles. To solve the problem, the company decided to build a Texas-size reservoir to hold the black gold.

After selecting a site in adjacent Ward County southeast of Monahans and not far from the Texas & Pacific main line, Roxana brought in an army of workmen to dig a giant hole. More men than the nearby town could accommodate, the workforce lived in tents near the job site.

Using mule-drawn equipment, the workers completed an excavation that from an airplane must have looked like a wide meteor crater. Next workers laid wire mesh over the packed earth. Then, working twenty-four hours a day, contractors started pouring tons of concrete. When the concrete cured, the tank measured 522.6 feet from north to south and 426.6 feet east to west. With forty-five-degree walls, the tank dropped 36.0 feet from roof to floor at the center and 25.0 feet along the perimeter.

A story provided to the *Dallas Morning News* by a correspondent in San Angelo and published February 19, 1928, said company officials reported the cost of the tank as $250,000—a quarter a barrel in storage costs compared to fifty cents a barrel for storage in steel tanks.

By late April 1928, workers hammered away at a wooden cover for the colossal tank, placing creosote-soaked support timbers at fourteen-foot intervals across the sprawling reservoir floor. Those timbers supported a domed redwood roof covered with tarpaper.

Pressurized crude entered into the bottom of the tank, the intake located near a huge drain that would be used to empty the tank in case of fire. The tank also had six 150-foot lightning rods rising from it.

One thing Roxana's engineers apparently forgot to take into consideration was the weight of crude. One gallon of the thick stuff weighs about 8 pounds. A barrel of oil contains forty-two gallons and weighs some 336 pounds. When Roxana injected one million barrels of oil into the tank, the weight bearing down on the concrete amounted to 870 pounds per square foot. Consisting of seamed sections of concrete, under that much pressure the tank leaked. Beyond that, despite the roof, evaporation also claimed oil. Also, the weight of the roof put additional stress on the concrete.

Even so, the loss happened slowly enough to make the tank workable for a time. The oil it did manage to hold got shipped by rail to Oklahoma to be refined. But when production near Wink began to decline, the flow from the field could be more easily moved by traditional methods.

Not long after the economy soured following the stock market crash in October 1929, Roxana stopped using its below-ground coliseum without seats. In the early 1930s, the company removed and sold the wood. According to Ben White, retired Monahans High School swim coach and local history buff, quite a few board feet of the lumber ended up in residences and buildings in Monahans.

The huge concrete hole in the ground, wider than five football fields, lay abandoned and mostly forgotten until 1954, when Monahans officials tried to get the tank and land around it for a city park. Shell nixed a lease agreement but said it would sell the property. The city opted not to buy it, but a former city employee named Wayne Long did. He envisioned the tank awash with a fluid then even more precious than crude oil—fresh water.

Long drilled six water wells to fill the tank, turned a cut that had been made to remove the timbers into a boat ramp and transformed the million-barrel oil reservoir into a million-barrel lake—the most water they'd seen in one place since moving to West Texas from Corpus Christi in 1950. Their lake would be a place where people could swim, ski and fish in the middle of a semi-desert.

For the lake's grand opening in 1958, Long and his wife, Amalie, brought in a pair of professional water skiers from Austin to crisscross their new waterhole.

But the lake didn't hold water any better than oil and soon disappeared, along with all the money the Longs had sunk into the project. Not a man to give up easily, Long spent a bunch more on engineering fees hoping to find and fix the source of the leak.

Despite Long's best efforts, tests showed the reservoir still leaked. An attempt to transform the tank into an automobile racetrack also foundered. Finally, he gave up on a literal and figurative dry hole. According to local lore, his failure sent him into an emotional downward spiral that ended with his death of a heart attack in 1980.

Six years later, Amalie Long donated the tank and 14.5 acres around it to the Ward County Historical Commission for use as a museum complex and park. After nearly sixty years, someone had finally come up with an idea that held water.

The Yates Hotel

Rankin Museum Association president Donna Bell has spent much of her life on a ranch and is not afraid of hard work. When money became available to repaint the lobby of Rankin's old Yates Hotel, now the town's museum, she pitched in and helped prep the plaster walls for a color makeover. But she encountered a stubborn raised spot next to the stairs that she couldn't budge no matter how hard she tried. Finally, she gave up and just painted over it.

Later, from one of the sons of hotel builder Ira Yates, the legendary father of the old rich Yates Field, she learned the story behind that rough place in the wall. It marked a rough time in Rankin's history when bootleg booze and black gold flowed with equal ease.

Yates built the three-story, forty-six-room sandy brick hotel in 1927 at the height of the oil boom that exploded on the Pecos County ranch he had traded a general store for in 1915. In considering a name for his new hostelry, he modestly thought Yates Hotel had a nice ring to it.

"He kept an upstairs room," Mrs. Bell says. "We haven't identified which room, but he played a lot of poker in it."

Billed as the first fireproof hotel between Fort Worth and El Paso, the Yates had a restaurant, drugstore and barbershop. The hotel saw many a handshake deal during the boom years and became a popular stopping place for east–west travelers. The rooms on the north side had no closets and cost less than the south-side rooms, which caught a better breeze and had a door between rooms so they could be used as suites. North or south side, however, guests had to walk down the hall to a bathroom.

By today's standards, a room on either side of the hotel did not cost all that much. A single schoolteacher who lived there in the late 1930s paid thirty-nine dollars a month for a room—meals included.

"There's a cute story about an old maid (probably all of twenty-five to thirty years old) Home Extension agent from Austin who used to stay at the Yates in the '40s," Mrs. Bell says. "She always washed her stockings at night and hung them in the bathroom to dry. One morning she came in and found some man had washed his socks and hung them right next to her hose. She was scandalized."

The hotel closed in 1964 and stood vacant for a decade before the Rankin Museum Association converted it into a museum. Though someone vandalized the hotel about a year after it went out of business, the Yates's original wicker furniture still sits in the lobby with its restored black and white checkerboard floor.

During the Yates's heyday, within an easy walk from the hotel lay one of the marvels of West Texas: Rankin Beach. That part of the state had not had any waterfront access since prehistoric times, but Yates put in a giant concrete swimming hole, 60 feet wide and 120 feet long. Legend has it that he even had beach sand trucked in from the Texas coast, though he could have gotten plenty from the sand dunes of not-too-distant Ward County.

Built during Rankin's oil boom years, the old Yates Hotel stood abandoned before it began a new life as a museum. *Photo by Mike Cox.*

People could keep cool in Yates's pool, enjoy live entertainment at the adjoining dance pavilion or spin around on a skating rink. A young accordion player named Lawrence Welk and his orchestra played at Rankin Beach in 1928–29, as did Louis Armstrong and Jack Teagarden.

One night during the boom, while her husband toiled away in the oil patch, his pretty wife sashayed and shimmied on the dance floor at the nearby Skidmore Plantation with an equally light-footed male partner. The evening seemed magical until the woman's husband showed up and pulled a pistol from his oil-stained coveralls. Seeking any port in a storm, the woman and her dancing partner hoofed it toward the Yates Hotel, the armed husband close behind. When they entered the hotel's lobby, the bellhop ducked as the husband fired several shots at the man he'd caught dancing with his wife.

None of the bullets took effect, and officers soon corralled the jealous husband, but the flying lead left some ugly pockmarks in the wall. For some reason, whoever repaired the bullet holes did not bother to smooth over the one next to the stairway. So far as is known, that was the only gunplay at the Yates. That may be why the hotel has a scarcity of ghosts.

Almost all old hotels come furnished with at least one restless spirit, but Mrs. Bell says the Yates is no Hotel California. One woman claimed to have had encounters with a lady apparition she called Gertrude, but Mrs. Bell says she's never heard or seen anything unusual at the Yates other than the old bullet hole.

If anyone's spirit is lingering at the Yates, by all rights it ought to be Yates himself. He spent a lot of time in his hotel prior to his death in 1939, and oil paintings of him and his wife are prominently displayed in the lobby.

For a fellow who didn't learn to read until he was fourteen, Yates obviously had a good head for business. Folks said he did well at cards, too. "He insisted that all his children learn to play poker," Mrs. Bell says. "He said poker would make them good at business."

Knowing when to fold 'em and when to hold 'em sure paid off for the old man.

PANSY CARPENTER

The old woman walked along one of McCamey's unpaved streets, pulling a red Radio Flyer wagon. Occasionally she stooped to pick up a tin can or some other piece of junk as she shuffled along, checking garbage bins for food.

Pansy Carpenter lived in a scrap-lumber shack in an oil town that, like her, had seen its better days. But inside her home stood a piano, and on that piano sat framed photographs reminding her of what had been and what might have been, including a Mary Pickford–like portrait of a beautiful young woman. That woman looked like a silent movie star, her blonde hair flowing like a golden waterfall, cascading in long curls down bare shoulders. Cream-faced, she had a sly smile and moist, knowing eyes. No wonder some young man fell hopelessly in love with her and asked her to marry him. No wonder she said yes to someone as handsome as she was lovely.

Though her looks could have given her a shot at Hollywood, Pansy opted for the circus world. She and her husband had a trapeze act in a traveling show. They drew big crowds and made good money. All that changed in a moment.

Following the 1925 discovery of shallow oil in what became West Texas's Yates Field, McCamey grew from just a name printed on a plat to a town of ten thousand by September 1926. With money flowing almost as freely as gushing crude, Pansy's circus troupe came to McCamey and set up its big top at the edge of town.

Pansy Carpenter came to McCamey during the oil boom and stayed there the rest of her life. *Author's collection.*

One night, as hundreds watched, Pansy and her husband toppled from the high wire. If the circus hands had a net up, it did not work. The fall killed her husband, and though Pansy survived, she had suffered a head injury. Either due to that trauma or grief or both, she was never the same.

Pansy could have gone home to her family in Medina County, where she grew up and attended school, but she opted to stay in McCamey. She and her husband had motored into town in his new Model A, a vehicle she never learned to drive. But she kept the Ford as a monument to her late husband, setting its wheels in concrete so it couldn't be stolen.

That's the story McCamey old-timers used to tell, but there's little on the record to back it up. Newspapers of the day devoted ample coverage to McCamey's development, but a search of a newspaper database with millions of digitized pages does not turn up anything on a circus performer dying there or any mention of a performer named Pansy Carpenter. Nor do cemetery lists reveal any graves in Upton County that might be the final resting place of her husband, assuming his last name was Carpenter.

It may be that McCamey was in such a frenzy of prosperity at the time that no one thought it a particularly big deal for a strikingly glamorous young trapeze artist, tragically widowed, to have gotten marooned in a West Texas boom town. "Who knows what the truth is?" the author of the *Pictorial History of Upton County* asked rhetorically in a half-page devoted to Pansy. The book contains the portrait of Pansy at the height of her career and two other images.

Apparently as handy with saw and hammer as she had been adroit on the ropes, Pansy built her own small house with an attached garage. That's where she kept the Model A. No longer able to make a living as a performer, she survived by throwing up and decorating shacks she rented to oil field workers. No slumlord, she sewed curtains, built trellis-shaded porches and turned flattened tin into architectural ornaments. When housing grew particularly tight, she also converted stripped-down car bodies into rental property, replacing missing doors or windows with wood.

A recycler before the word came into use, Pansy pulled her wagon all over town as she scavenged anything she felt could be repurposed—boards, boxes, corrugated metal, tin, cans, bottle caps, vehicle parts and oil field items. Someone later recalled that she once walked all the way to San Angelo, pulling her wagon, to buy a commode.

Early on she must have had to fight off amorous roughnecks and drillers, but that no longer posed a problem as her beauty faded with the passing years. Another photograph, taken when she was forty, shows that she had shortened her hair, which had long since reverted to its natural brown. Her cheeks gaunt, it looks like she didn't get the best of dental care. The older she grew, the more reclusive she became.

Children were afraid of her, but those who knew her realized she posed no danger. In fact, while she often fished food from trash cans behind grocery stores or cafés, she frequently shared her bounty with people even worse off.

In failing health and no longer able to live alone, in May 1972 she sold her long-dead husband's old car and went home to Medina County and what family she had left. Five months later, on October 28, she died in a Kerrville hospital at seventy-eight.

Her short obituary offered a few more details on her life. She was born in Indian Territory (Oklahoma) on January 6, 1894, though her family soon moved to Texas. She had a brother in California, a sister in Oregon and a half brother in San Antonio. Her death certificate shows her father's name was Virgil L. Bennett, but the obituary gave her brother's last name as Carr.

McCamey's Mendoza Trail Museum has on display one of Pansy's wagons, some of her photographs and a collection of the artwork she created from found items. Two hundred forty-five miles to the east, Pansy is buried in Medina County's Oak Rest Cemetery, her simple grave marker revealing only her date of birth and death.

Treasure Tales

BILL NARD'S LOST LEAD MINE

As an old man, Henry Smith liked to tell folks about the lost mine. He'd spent a fair amount of time in his younger years looking for it, but he never found it. Smith's search was not for the granddaddy of all lost Texas mines, the Spanish silver works Jim Bowie supposedly found in the early 1830s somewhere near the old mission in Menard County. Folks are still searching for that mine, but the other old mine pretty much has been forgotten. The lead mine.

Lead is not the most precious of minerals, but along the Texas frontier it ranked as a pretty important item when muzzleloading rifles and pistols fired homemade lead balls. Lead for bullet molding could be bought, of course, but a handy vein of ore saved money and time.

Llano County pioneer Billy Nard discovered a lead vein and began working it in the 1860s. With the Indians taking advantage of the fact that most of the menfolk were off fighting Yankees, a steady lead supply was particularly vital in areas prone to moonlight raids. In fact, when Comanches came calling, lead suddenly became more valuable than gold.

No prospector, Nard made a simple living as a bee hunter. He wasn't interested in bees per se, but they led him to honeycombs. He gathered and sold honey. His wife later recalled that when in search of honey he usually left their cabin with a sack over his shoulder, a hatchet on his belt and his muzzleloader in his hands. Nard came home with honey often enough to make ends meet. Less frequently, based on need, he returned to their homestead with a sack full of lead ore.

Nard molded bullets from the melted ore and shared the lead with his neighbors. He sold honey but never charged anyone for the lead. A man could live without honey, but at this stage of Texas's history, bullets were no luxury. Despite his willingness to share his ore, Nard carefully guarded the location of his mine. He didn't even tell his wife, though he promised to tell his children before he died.

Unfortunately, that death came sooner than Nard or anyone in his family expected. Indians killed him, but not directly. Nard was hunting wild hogs with one of his boys and his brother-in-law on Silver Creek, a tributary of Sandy Creek, when Indians surprised the party. Grabbing up his nine-year-old son, Nard ran hell-for-leather toward his cabin. In doing so, he slogged through deep sand in the creek bed. Stout to the point of fleshiness, Nard escaped the Indians red faced and panting. For whatever the reason, he had opted flight over using some of the bullets from his secret lead mine.

Two days later, untouched by arrow or bullet, Nard died, probably of a heart attack triggered by the shock of the encounter coupled with the exertion of his run. The location of his lead honey hole died with him.

Some people in Llano County were still telling the story of the lost lead mine as late as the 1940s. One of the tellers was Smith, whose uncle was Nard's brother-in-law. As a youngster, Smith helped his father mold bullets from the ore supplied by Nard. He recalled that the lead made suitable bullets, but it was not of the quality that could be purchased.

After Nard died, his widow and children moved in with the Smith family. When Henry Smith got old enough to prowl around by himself, he tried without success to find the lost mine. His best guess, based on where Nard had his cabin, was that the ore vein lay somewhere near Sandy Creek. Others said it was near Cedar Mountain, while some maintained the mine was along Honey Creek.

Smith wasn't the only one interested in finding the mine. For a long time, Llano County rancher Tom Moore had a standing offer of $500 for the person who found it, but no one ever collected the reward.

JOE PRUNO'S GOLD

His gray beard obscuring most of his weathered face and hanging untrimmed all the way to his sweat-stained belt, the small Frenchman traveled from ranch to ranch in Martin County in an old covered wagon pulled by two mules and followed by a couple of dogs.

The story of Joe A. Pruno reads like a Victorian-era dime novel, complete with ample exaggeration, outright fabrication and historical inaccuracies. For preserving the tale, fanciful and disjointed as it is, one Otto Fisher deserves a tip of the Stetson. At some point after meeting him in 1922 on the Stokes Ranch, Fisher wrote down Pruno's recollections, putting them in first person. A fifteen-page typescript of the document ended up in the Martin County museum in Stanton.

Pruno told Fisher he came into the world on April 1, 1842, in one of France's African colonies. His mother died of a fever shortly after his birth. A sea captain, his father brought him to the United States at age twelve. On the way across the ocean, their vessel survived a severe storm. "We landed somewhere on the Southern coast," he told Fisher. "I had two aunts in America and I mixed with these aunts at times but I had a job most of the time on river boats; did dish washing and learned to cook."

He said he enlisted in the Union army during the Civil War, serving under the flamboyant George Armstrong Custer. About all Pruno had to say of his military experience was that "we tramped up hills, in ditches and in the rain."

After the war, he continued, he married and settled in Chicago. He worked as a railroad fireman, stoking boilers on steam locomotives. When their home burned near the end of the 1860s, the couple moved to Ozark Lake, Missouri. He left his wife there and enlisted to serve once more under Custer. Having risen to the rank of major general of volunteers during the Civil War, Custer returned to the regular army at reduced rank. By 1866, however, he was a lieutenant colonel in command of the Seventh Cavalry. The "boy general," as he was called, served in Indian Territory through 1873, when the Seventh went to the Black Hills of North Dakota.

Pruno said while riding as a scout for Custer in what is now Oklahoma the Indians captured him and took him into Texas. (This is doubtful. Hostile Indians usually captured only women and children, preferring to kill and scalp the menfolk.) They went as far as the future location of Midland, he said. The military rescued him after about six months.

Granted a leave from the army, Pruno went to California to hunt gold. He claimed he found a lot of the precious metal somewhere near Sacramento, selling nuggets and the rights to his dig for a considerable sum.

Discharged from the army in 1872, he headed east to Ozark City with a fortune in gold coin. His two burros heavily laden, he took a circuitous route through the territories of Arizona and New Mexico into West Texas, dodging Indians and traveling from water hole to water hole while living off buffalo and antelope. In what later became Stanton County, he said he decided to bury the larger portion of his gold in one location, with a lesser amount hidden at another point.

After spending some time at Fort Concho, Pruno said he traveled back to Missouri, where he claimed his wife had been captured by Indians. (Except for the James and Dalton boys, the Show Me State was pretty tame by then. This is probably another of the windy parts of his story.)

In 1875, not having found his wife, Pruno returned to Texas and tried to locate his hidden treasure. Alas, despite his best efforts to make the trove findable, he never rediscovered his horde. Naturally, he spent most of the rest of his life looking for it.

Giving up his long-distance rambling, he stayed in the Lone Star State, working on various ranches, including making concrete water troughs and putting up windmills on the storied Slaughter Ranch. He also hauled freight from the Texas & Pacific Railroad to Ballinger, Brady and Fredericksburg. For a time in the early 1900s, he got hired as a laborer during the construction of the Galveston sea wall.

In addition to losing his treasure, Pruno managed to find and lose three wives. He fathered seven children, three of his daughters serving as nurses during World War I.

Stanton resident Cliff Hazelwood remembers seeing Pruno when he was a kid. He heard stories about the old man but never got a chance to talk to him. "I think that gold is still right there where he buried it," Hazelwood says.

Pruno, who eventually moved to Stanton, died in July 1942 at more than one hundred years old, assuming he had told the truth about his date of birth. Fisher said the old man was buried in the town's Catholic cemetery. If he ever had a tombstone, it has not been located. Neither has his treasure.

Necessities

"WHEN YOU GET RIGHT THIRSTY…"

Carr Spraberry, who came to Jones County in the fall of 1879, knew what it was like to be thirsty. Years after the fact, a ride he made from near present-day Anson to Fort Phantom Hill to fetch a doctor for a sick woman still stood out in his mind. He didn't say what time of year he made the ride, but it must have been summer. "I became very thirsty and really suffered," he recalled.

After a time in the saddle, he rode into a hollow and saw a profusion of cow trails. "'Must be water near,' I said to myself. The trails got bigger and bigger, and finally I found water. I knelt down at the pool and drank, and stayed half an hour, taking two more swigs of water." The water enabled him to continue his mercy mission.

"A day or two later I met a man who asked me how many dead cows there were at that pool. 'I saw none and tasted none,' said I. Said the man, 'There are nine dead cows in that pool, and it was not over 20 steps long.'"

Spraberry's next drink came from the Clear Fork of the Brazos. "I got to the river," he said. "Drank more water. When you get right thirsty for water, I'll tell you, any water is good. I know; for, as you see, I have tried it."

From the river Spraberry still had another four-mile ride to Fort Phantom Hill. And when he got there he discovered that the doctor had ridden to Albany on another emergency. Some helpful soul suggested that lacking a doctor, Spraberry should bring the sick woman mustard (for plasters), spirits of nitrate and Tutt's pills. Stuffing the frontier medicine into his saddlebag, he left at sundown on his return journey, "and I rode a good horse down on the trip."

His thirst and hard riding proved to have been all for naught. "I got back at break of day," he recalled. "They had just laid Mrs. Riley out."

Spraberry got one good night's sleep before he had to make another trip to Phantom Hill. This time he rode in a wagon with his brother-in-law to buy a coffin for their aunt, who had died from an attack of colic. On their way, they met the preacher on his way back from Phantom Hill with a coffin for Mrs. Riley.

The woman Spraberry had tried to get a doctor for had the distinction of being the first person buried in Anson's Mount Hope Cemetery. Spraberry's aunt, Mollie Carr, was the second.

Spraberry had not been able to save Mrs. Riley, but in a way, he had been lucky. Along the Texas frontier, bad water posed just about as much of a problem as no or little water.

The common perception is that Indians posed the greatest threat to settlers and U.S. soldiers stationed along Texas's western frontier. But that's wrong. Mindless enemies of another sort lurked around all the army's forts, ready to kill the unwary. They could not be seen, which made them hard to fight.

Water is necessary to sustain life, but in West Texas, it could also kill you. *Author's collection.*

Fort Concho, established along the Concho River in 1867, guarded that part of the frontier for more than twenty years. Comanche and Kiowa Indians posed a definite threat to the soldiers stationed there, especially during the post's earlier years. But the soldiers faced a deadlier foe—bad water. In October 1870, the post surgeon reported thirty-five cases of typhoid fever, sixty-nine cases of acute diarrhea and dysentery and twenty-one cases identified as "continued and remittent fever." Six soldiers died that month from one or another of those ailments.

The doctor may or may not have had a microscope at his disposal, but he knew the culprit: tainted water. A year before, he had reported that the North Concho River at that time consisted of only shallow, stagnant pools. The main arm of the river, he said, had been contaminated with putrefying animal matter, including buffalo carcasses. River water smelled bad and tasted worse.

Indeed, when the river was low it teemed with harmful microbes, the invisible life forms that could kill a man as surely as a red-painted Comanche arrow or a spiraling .50-caliber slug from a Spencer carbine.

Living on the frontier wasn't easy, but it wasn't too hard to die.

Pass Them Biscuits, Please

Remember the biscuit scene in John Wayne's *McLintock*? Chill Wills, playing rancher George Washington McLintock's right-hand man in the 1963 western comedy, says to McLintock (Wayne): "You wanna see sumthin' that came directly from heaven?"

Wills then hands Wayne a golden-topped biscuit. The Duke looks at it for a moment before cautiously taking a bite.

"Where'd you get this?" he asks.

"That boy's mamma baked 'em," Wills replies, pointing to a strapping farm boy (Patrick Wayne) and his beautiful mother. "You thinkin' the same thing I'm thinkin'?"

Wills introduces McLintock to the widow Louise Warren, played by Yvonne de Carlo. "Ma'am, he has a few choice things to say about your biscuits."

Wayne looks uncomfortable, lost for words. Finally he blurts: "Well… they're great!" And the lady who is not only pretty but can make heavenly biscuits gets hired on the spot as McLintock's new cook.

Good biscuits have that kind of power. A pioneer in what is now Tarrant County once pacified some potentially hostile Indians by, in the Texas vernacular,

West Texas cowboys enjoyed biscuits prepared at the back of chuck wagons like this one. *Author's collection.*

cooking them up a mess of what must have been darn tasty biscuits. Their bellies full, the Indians had no bone to pick with a man who could cook like that.

Back then, flour stood in short supply and came at a high price. Most early-day Texans got by quite well on corn bread, with flour-made biscuits a rare treat. When flour eventually became more readily available, biscuits became a Texas staple as well. Chuck wagon cooks baked cow-camp biscuits in Dutch ovens, and families enjoyed "from scratch" biscuits at home.

My grandmother, born in West Texas in the spring of 1898, learned to cook before foods came in ready-to-mix boxes and long before ready-to-bake or ready-to-microwave dishes. Making biscuits to go with a meal (old Texans would eat biscuits with any meal, not just breakfast) came as easily to her as zapping instant macaroni and cheese is for someone today.

Not only could Grandmother quickly put hot biscuits on the table, they tasted wonderful. Slathering them in real butter and covering them with honey, molasses or homemade pear preserves added to the pleasure—and calorie content—of her biscuits.

Sadly, routinely making biscuits the old-fashioned way is as rare today as flour used to be. The art has been mostly relegated to recreational chuck wagon cooks and commercial cowboy breakfast operations.

Back when or now, cooking biscuits involves more than combining the ingredients and baking the result. As the *McLintock* scene suggests, good biscuits almost do seem divinely inspired.

Biscuits, by accident or design, also could do the devil's work. "My grandfather's family lived in Washington and Grimes Counties," recalls *Polk County Enterprise* editor Valerie Reddell. "His dad had the general store in North Zulch. On several occasions I heard a story about Aunt Hen (which I assumed was Great-Granddad's aunt) making biscuits for a big family dinner. Aunt Hen must not have been big on reading labels, because when she was supposed to add baking powder to the biscuits, she added in a goodly amount of rat poison. The recipe took a heavy toll on the biscuit eaters."

In their 1891 book *On a Mexican Mustang Through Texas*, authors Alex Sweet and John A. Knox devoted a paragraph to the art of biscuit making. "Either of us could prepare or mix the dough, put it in the skillet, put on the cover and set the skillet on the fire," they wrote, "but there was never any certainty as to what the skillet would produce."

Sometimes, they continued, "it would be a pudding, and at other times it would be a flour-and-water brick, hard enough to ruin the digestive organs of a camel." Their guide, on the other hand, always succeeded in making "splendid" biscuits. Not wanting to make him feel underappreciated, the two travelers allowed their guide to take over all the biscuit building, as they called it.

Light Crust flour made good biscuits and helped launch a political career. *Author's collection.*

Texas had no more famous brand of flour than the product bagged by the Burrus Mill and Elevator Co. of Fort Worth. While the company's name may not resonate, its product did: Light Crust Flour. To help sell its product, the mill sponsored a western swing band featuring one Bob Wills, later of "San Antonio Rose" fame. Company president was future Texas governor W. Lee "Pappy" O'Daniel.

A forty-eight-page recipe booklet produced by the mill in the mid-1930s, with "practical recipes" tested and approved by Mrs. Leonore Standifer, featured four biscuit formulas: Dixie Yeast Biscuits, Perfect Baking Powder Biscuits, Rose Biscuits (regular old biscuits made with red food coloring) and Sour Milk Biscuits. This is the Perfect Baking Powder recipe:

Scant cup sweet milk [translation: people used to call regular milk sweet milk to distinguish it from buttermilk]
2 cups Light Crust flour [sorry, the mill's long since been corporately absorbed]
3 teaspoons baking powder [Calumet was the old-time standard]
1 teaspoon salt
2 tablespoons shortening [trans fats weren't a factor in those days]

Sift Light Crust flour, baking powder and salt together into mixing bowl, after sifting flour once before measuring.
Push flour to sides of bowl, making a well in the center. Pour milk into well, put in the shortening, blend milk and shortening well together, adding all the flour. Blend thoroughly, but lightly. Put out on floured rolling board and fold over a few times to make smooth. Roll out to ½ inch in thickness, cut with small biscuit cutter and place in well greased shallow pans. Bake in quick over, 500 degrees, about five minutes.

The booklet continued, "These biscuits made of Light Crust flour will be delightfully fluffy and white and deliciously flavored."

Clearly, those biscuits must have been unlike those the late Texas writer Fred Gipson recalled from his early twentieth-century childhood. Some of the biscuits he remembered eating "squatted to rise and baked on the squat." As a youngster, Gipson and many other rural Texans in the early decades of the 1900s carried biscuit-and-bacon sandwiches to school each day. Their lunchbox was a lard bucket with holes punched in the top.

Back before World War I, Hattie Hester and her cousin Ola Mae attended a small school at Rochester, in West Texas. Annoyed at their teacher for some reason, they decided to get revenge. They had no particular form of retaliation in mind until they spotted a dead frog in the road as they walked to school. "We decided to make a sandwich with a biscuit from our lunch," Hattie later recalled. "We put the dead frog-and-biscuit sandwich on his desk. If he ever found out who did it, we didn't know it."

That would have been one biscuit that did not look like something from heaven.

Weather Wonders

THE DAY THE CATFISH FROZE

In the days before instantly available color weather radar, Isaac Cline's story sounded like a Texas-size whopper. Cline had been assigned to Fort Concho in the spring of 1885 as the officer in charge of the army's Signal Service station. He oversaw the West Texas cavalry post's telegraph service, which constituted the only real-time link to the outside world from that part of the state. He also took daily weather observations.

One day that August, he routinely wired his climate report to Washington, D.C. Conditions at the fort were hot and dry. Nothing else going on, Cline walked from the fort to the small town on the other side of the Concho River, San Angelo. As he crossed the footbridge over the summer-sluggish stream, he heard a loud roar. At first he thought it could be distant thunder, but the sky was clear in every direction. As he pondered the possibilities, a wall of water nearly twenty feet high suddenly appeared upstream.

Running for his life, Cline made it over the bridge in time to beat the roiling flood surge heading in his direction, but a man crossing the river in a carriage was not as lucky. As Cline watched in horror, a watery cliff crashed into the wagon, sending it and its occupant tumbling downstream.

That was shocking, but what Cline saw next was simply bizarre. No matter the tragedy that had just unfolded, men soon began gathering along the river and pulling big fish from the water. When a two-foot catfish drifted by, motivated both by curiosity and the thought of fresh fried fish, Cline reached

Meteorologist Isaac Cline (1861–1955). *Author's collection.*

into the water to grab the big whisker fish. What happened then stunned the young army scientist both literally and figuratively: the water was freezing cold.

On a scorching summer day, something had chilled the water to the extent that it had incapacitated the fish as surely as if someone had tossed a stick of dynamite into the river. Cline landed his dinner, but it took him a while longer to learn what had caused the sudden temperature drop in the Concho.

The Signal Corps officer later found out that a giant thunderstorm had pounded West Texas about fifty miles above San Angelo, dropping hail the size of ostrich eggs. Leaving spheres of ice piled in three-foot drifts, the barrage from above killed thousands of cattle. Hail-chilled runoff from the intense supercell well beyond the horizon had put the Concho on the rise and claimed several lives along the suddenly swollen stream.

Though that 1885 storm proved deadly for people and fish along the Concho River, only rarely does hail ever kill people. But of only three known hail fatalities in the United States, two have happened in Texas: one in the early 1930s, the other on March 28, 2000, when one of three victims of a tornado that struck Fort Worth died after being struck by a grapefruit-sized hailstone.

Realizing the highly unusual nature of the weather-caused fish kill he had observed, Cline wrote an article on the storm and its aftereffect for the *Monthly Weather Review*, a government publication. To Cline's great annoyance, the editor rejected the story as just another fanciful Texas brag. But Cline was not from Texas, and he had both experienced the frigid river water and seen the stunned fish. To back up his claim, he checked the records and located a documented report from the summer of 1877 in which hailstones as big as oranges had killed a herd of ponies in Wyoming's Yellowstone Valley. He also found three other storms reported in 1881–82 that left high drifts of giant hailstones.

Despite a temporary setback caused by a wild hail storm, the Concho River continued to produce good-size catfish. *Author's collection*.

Cline stayed at San Angelo until March 1889, when the army ordered his transfer to another weather station: the Signal Corps facility at the busy port of Galveston. When Congress created the Weather Bureau in 1890, Cline left the army and became Galveston's first civilian meteorologist. Ten years later, he was the official who tried to warn the island city of the approaching hurricane that resulted in what still stands as the nation's deadliest natural disaster.

Forty-five years later, he told that story—along with the Concho catfish tale—in his memoir, *Storms, Floods and Sunshine.*

El Paso's Big Blow

Even under normal circumstances, no one could label El Paso a city in the midst of a tropical rain forest. In a good year, which is to say an average year, the city at the Pass of the North enjoys only nine inches of rain. But in the spring of 1895, what fell from the sky was dust. Late on the night of April 4, a Thursday, a powerful early spring cold front began blowing through El Paso.

"A Big Blow," read the headline of the *El Paso Times* the next afternoon. "El Paso Is Visited by a Terrific Wind and Sand Storm. Much Damage Done."

By midnight, the anemometer at the Weather Bureau registered fifty miles an hour, and the wind "continued to gain strength" beyond that until 11:00 a.m. that April 5.

People talked about El Paso's April 5, 1895 "Big Blow" for years. *Author's collection.*

Calling the weather "decidedly cyclonic," the newspaper reported that El Pasoans and visitors "had to desert the streets to avoid the storm of pebbles and sand that beat them in the face and almost swept them off their feet."

The wind ripped the roof from two large building at the smelter and then "dashed on down the river to El Paso where it played havoc with roofs, awnings and signs." The Vendome Hotel lost its roof "with a rip and roar, fragments flying in every direction." The courthouse tower "bent before the gale like the mast of a ship and the occupants of the building watched its gyrations with no small show of trepidation." Signs, awnings, and pieces of roofs became deadly projectiles, though the newspaper reported no injuries connected to the storm. That's probably because government offices curtailed their activities, schools and many businesses closed and the streetcar line quit running.

"A lady passing up Oregon Street lost control of her wearing apparel which turned wrong side out—so to speak—like a refractory umbrella," the newspaper noted. "But the wind filled the eyes of the naughty men with sand and they could not look."

The wind took down many of the city's scarce trees and ripped away telegraph, telephone and power lines, leaving the city without electric lights.

At 4:30 p.m. that Friday, the wind finally calmed. By nightfall, the sky had cleared and the temperature had begun to fall. "At midnight," the newspaper concluded, "the weather was real chilly and the streets were completely deserted except by the police."

Local newspapers concentrated on what happened in El Paso, but the cold front and resulting sandstorm swept from the northwest across much of Texas, taking down line shacks along the Texas & Pacific Railroad and wreaking considerable havoc across the state. In fact, not until the Dust Bowl days of the 1930s would Texas see such a severe spate of sandstorms.

The early April storm made news all across the Central Plains. In the high country of Colorado, it brought snow and dust. One newspaper reported that "trains were stalled on all the railway lines east of Denver and hundreds of men and several snow plows are engaged in clearing the tracks of drifting snow and sand." South of the Snow Belt, another newspaper reported, "The sun was frequently so obscured by sand as to necessitate the lighting of lamps."

The storm lasted nearly two full days. In the Panhandle and elsewhere on the Great Plains, the unusually powerful front took a heavy toll on stockmen. "The storm came so suddenly that few people got their stock in," a Kansas newspaper told its readers. "Thousands of dollars worth of stock…was lost…Some estimate the loss at 50 per cent while others claim 25 per cent will cover the loss."

A severe drought compounded the effect of the powerful wind associated with the cold front. "Unless it rains soon many more [animals] will perish," the newspaper continued, "as the grass is so completely covered with the mud the stock can not eat it." Indeed, by April 17, even Austin, which normally gets nearly three feet of rain a year, had recorded only three inches of precipitation.

The drought broke later that spring, and the state did not endure another prolonged dry spell until well into the twentieth century.

TEACHER RODE A TORNADO

School teaching has never been the best-paying avocation, but the terms of employment have definitely improved over the last century.

When the Haskell County community of Marcy made the decision in 1906 to relocate three miles to be on the right of way of the new Kansas City, Mexico and Orient Railroad, A.B. Carothers donated the land for the new tracks and 160 acres for the town site. In appreciation, the railroad gave him first choice on what the new town should be called. He thought Carothers, Texas, would be a fine name, but a check with postal authorities determined that handle had already been taken in Texas. Not being able to honor the Haskell County landowner, the railroad opted to call the new town Rochester, after Rochester, New York. His altruistic spirit not dampened, Carothers paid for construction of a one-room schoolhouse. Classes began in the fall with nine grades and one teacher.

These children went to school in the Haskell County community of New Mid, only four miles from Rochester. The 1907 tornado just missed their town but devastated the Rochester school where Kate Finley taught. *Author's collection.*

Weather Wonders

According to Marguerite Gauntt and Modelle Ballard's 1976 history of Rochester, *When the Rails Were Laid*, these were the teacher's conditions of employment:

- You will not marry during the term of your contract.
- You are not to keep company with men.
- You must be home between the hours of 3 p.m. and 6 a.m., unless attending a school function.
- You may not loiter downtown in ice cream stores.
- You may not travel beyond the city limits, unless you have permission of the chairman of the [school] board.
- You may not ride in a carriage or automobile with any man, unless he is your father or brother.
- You may not smoke cigarettes.
- You may not dress in bright colors.
- You may under no circumstances dye your hair.
- You must wear at least two petticoats.
- Your dresses must not be any shorter than two inches above the ankle.
- To keep the school room neat and clean, you must: sweep the floor once a day; scrub the floor once a week with hot soapy water; clean the blackboards once a day; start the fire at 7 a.m. so the room will be warm by 8 a.m.

Rochester's first teacher managed to abide by the school board's strict rules, but something else would seriously affect her enthusiasm for teaching in West Texas. In the predawn hours of July 2, 1907, Kate Slotton Finley, the town's young schoolteacher, lay sound asleep, peacefully abiding by her school board–imposed curfew, when her landlady woke her up. A bad storm was coming, she said. They needed to head for the storm cellar.

Either too sleepy or too confident, the teacher opted to stay in bed. Just about the time she got comfortably back to sleep, oblivious to the lightning flashes and the wildly turning public windmill in the middle of Rochester's main street, a tornado struck, tearing the roof off the boardinghouse. The rotating wind pulled Finley out of her bed, along with the heavy trunk containing most of her wardrobe. If she thought for a second that she was having a dream about flying, she soon realized she was moving through the night sky for real, her screams drowned in the roar of the wind.

Accounts of the storm do not reveal whether Finley consulted with her higher power while swirling in the air, but the winds set her down on Rochester's muddy street. Regaining consciousness, she began to crawl for help, blood rushing from a cut on her forehead. A local woman saw her and helped her to safety, finding her only injuries to be the cut and a dislocated thumb.

"I could see the church [across the street from her boardinghouse] swaying to and fro," the teacher later recalled in describing her brief ride on the wind. "I saw my trunk up in the air. I hit the ground flat, my bed sheet wrapped around me, and wringing wet."

The violent summer storm marked the end of Finley's teaching career in Rochester. The tornado had demolished her school and destroyed or damaged thirteen other structures in town, including the Methodist church. Besides, as the authors of the community history reported, Finley's close call left her "too nervous to teach."

Did John Roan Carve His Own Tombstone?

On December 13, 1879, the *Atlanta Constitution* published a brief story that should have been big news in Texas, but somehow no editor in the Lone Star State picked up on the Georgia daily's report. The story dealt with the purported solution of a twenty-nine-year-old mystery in central Texas: the disappearance of one John Roan.

In November 1879, the *Constitution* told its readers, someone exploring a cave near "Point Rock" in Lampasas County discovered a human skeleton inside. But there was more to the tale than that: "Near the skeleton was a rusty blade of a bowie knife, with the handle rotten with age. On a smooth limestone rock was carved in capital letters the following: 'I fell in here four days ago when the Indians were running me. I am starving. If Bill don't find me tomorrow I will run this knife through my heart. I can't stand to starve to death. John Roan.'" The date of the inscription was November 1, 1850.

The only other snippet of information the article included was this: "The cavern walls cannot be scaled without the aid of a rope twenty-five feet in length, and the aperture is exceedingly small. Roan's own efforts to save his own life would have been unavailing."

Like many interesting things I've run across over the years, I found this long-forgotten newspaper story by accident while looking online for something else. Intrigued, I immediately set about—pardon the expression—trying to flesh out the details of this skeleton tale. So far my efforts have proven fruitless.

—"I fell in here four days ago, when the Indians were running me. I am starving. If Bill don't find me to-morrow I will run this knife through my heart. I can't stand to starve to death. John Roan. November 1, 1850," was found recently in a cavern at Point. Rock, near Lampasas, Tenn. The message was carved in capital letters on the face of a smooth limestone rock. Near the rock was the skeleton of a man and near the skeleton the rusty blade of a bowie knife, the handle of which was rotten with age. The cavern walls cannot be scaled without the aid of a rope twenty-five feet in length, and the aperture is exceedingly small. Roan's own efforts to save his own life would have been unavailing.

This brief newspaper article from the 1870s is all that's known of John Roan. *Author's collection.*

For starters, a subscription website with thousands of old U.S. newspapers available for digital search reveals only one other contemporary news story about the discovery of the skeleton. That was in the *Vernon Clipper*, a newspaper published in Lamar County, Alabama. And that story, printed six days after the appearance of the first report, clearly is only a rewrite of the Atlanta article. No mention of Roan's bones can be found in any Texas newspaper.

On top of that, there's no community or landmark in Lampasas County called Point Rock. Over in East Texas there is a community in Grimes County called Roan's Prairie, which was named for one Willis I. Roan, an early settler from—interestingly enough—Alabama. He settled in the area that would bear his name in 1841. Judging from assorted genealogical websites, the Roan family flourished in Texas, and John is certainly a common given name.

But nowhere online or in any of various books on Lampasas County is there any mention of such a compelling story as a skeleton of a long-missing person being found in a cave. Nor do online listings of those lying in various Lampasas County cemeteries record a grave occupied by anyone named John Roan. (The county's Oak Hill Cemetery does have the final resting place of one Eddie Roan, who died at age twelve in 1948, but no other Roans are shown in any other cemetery in the county.)

Of course, it should be noted that in 1850, when Roan supposedly fell into a cave while being chased by Indians, Lampasas County did not yet exist as a political subdivision. In fact, the first settler did not put up a cabin in the vicinity of what would become Lampasas until 1853—three years after Roan supposedly met his fate. And it was three years after that before Lampasas County was organized.

But there were plenty of Indians in that part of Texas in 1850, and it's conceivable that Roan could have been in the area on a wild horse gathering expedition. Or maybe he had left the settlements to hunt buffalo or deer, which also were plentiful at the time. The Bill referred to in Roan's allegedly self-composed epitaph could have been the person hunting with him, perhaps having become separated from him when the Indians confronted them.

Lampasas County does have some limestone caves, particularly in Colorado Bend State Park, but one would think a cave with a carving such as described by the *Atlanta Constitution* story would be well known.

So, in 1879 did some bored journalist make up the story of John Roan's lonely suicide and the discovery of his remains nearly three decades later, or did it really happen?

LITTLE GIRL GRAVE

Surely her grieving parents wrote her name in their family Bible, noting the day she died on their way westward. Once, maybe, a wooden grave marker bore her name. But all that remains today is a mystery written in concrete: "Who is the little girl, age 3?"

At the foot of the small grave, located on the northern edge of County Road 185 in Comanche County about a mile and a half east of the ghost town of Sipe Springs, is a more modern granite marker with these additional words: "Little girl, age 3 died 1870, moving west." Those eight words sum up just about everything anyone living today knows about the lonely, rock-bordered grave.

Some say the little girl fell off the wagon and suffered a fatal head injury. Another story has her dying of disease, which seems more likely. Her family buried her where she died and then continued their journey.

Local folks at some point started putting flowers on the grave. Then someone offered a small toy. Over the years, that tradition has grown. Today, the grave is covered with toys, ceramic angels and kittens, coins, teddy bears, horseshoes, even a gimme cap. Periodically, a self-appointed local caretaker collects the money left at the grave and writes a check to the local volunteer fire department, but the toys and other items remain, fading in the sun.

Three years after the little girl's death, someone settled at a seeping spring a short distance west of her grave. The community came to be called Sipe Springs. It's pronounced "Seep" Springs, incidentally, not the way it's spelled. Whether that spelling was accidental or based on a variant acceptable in the nineteenth century remains open to discussion.

Unusual as its name is, Texas once had two places called Sipe Springs. The other, never as big as the one in Comanche County, was farther east in Milam County. A hundred years ago, it had a two-teacher school with three score students, but the school closed due to consolidation in 1931, and within a decade, nothing was left of the Milam County community.

Not that all that much is left of the Comanche County Sipe Springs. One old bank still stands. Someone has restored an old stone house that once stood in ruins. And there's the Masonic Hall, though it's a new one built when the original structure burned down not too long ago. West of the

People still leave toys and coins at Little Girl Grave. *Courtesy of Jerry Morgan.*

intersection that marks the center of the community are the ruins of an old saloon. Jerry Morgan, former owner of the *DeLeon Free Press*, said he found a late nineteenth-century nickel in the vicinity several years ago.

For a time in the late teens and early 1920s, a lot of nickels slid across the bar in and around Sipe Springs. Though named for water, the town got renewed vitality from the discovery of another liquid—oil.

Some say Sipe Springs had ten thousand residents for a time. Children crowded a large community school. Two banks did a flourishing business, as did numerous stores and eateries. When not busy earning money, local folks and roughnecks had entertainment choices ranging from an opera house to a professional baseball team. Soon the shallow oil field played out, and so did Sipe Springs. The government finally closed the post office in 1957, the boom days long gone.

Though Sipe Springs has had a minor population spurt from city folks buying country retreats, for years the only growth going on in Sipe Springs was at the cemetery. Land for the cemetery was donated in 1873, but for some reason, no one moved the little girl's grave to the site. In 1890, a wooden tabernacle went up, and the number of graves increased over the decades.

Imbedded in one granite marker in that cemetery are photographs of a young girl and boy labeled "Brother" and "Sister." On a seperate stone is inscribed "Marion Wayne Mote 1922–1937" and "Patty Mote 1925–1937." Also on the gravestone is this line: "Happy and gay, to school they went one day…They are not dead, just away." Though their gravestone doesn't say so, both children—originally from Comanche County—died in the March 18, 1937 New London school explosion in East Texas. That tragedy still stands as the nation's worst school disaster.

But the name of the child in Little Girl Grave remains a mystery.

Body in the Bale

Late summer and early fall is cotton ginning time in West Texas. Depending on a growing area's average temperatures, which of course vary from south to north, the annual process of transforming bolls to bales starts as early as July and extends into October.

Ever wonder how removing seeds from the fiber came to be called ginning? According to the Burton Cotton Gin Museum's website, after Eli Whitney invented the machine that transformed the industry in 1793, it came to be called "The Little Cotton Engine." Soon, "engine" got shortened to "gin," and a new noun entered the language.

Though most of the ginning is done by brainless machinery, the industry's human element has developed a colorful folklore with a range of subsets. But no ginning story can top the occasional tale of a body in a bale.

In 1909, an Erath County newspaper reported the grisly resolution of a missing child case. The previous fall, the newspaper said, a two-year-old boy had disappeared without a trace. He had last been seen playing near a cotton gin. The following spring, the toddler turned up in England—dead in a bale of fine Texas cotton.

Though admitting he got it secondhand, seventy-five-year-old James "Butterbean" ("I love butterbeans," he says, "but you just can't find 'em anymore") Carpenter offered another body-in-a-bale story. It supposedly happened during the 1950s somewhere in West Texas, possibly Ralls.

The Coleman County retiree, who raises miniature horses near Valera, related that his Uncle George's brother (his dad's sister's husband's brother) disappeared along with his elderly mother. The man had a reputation as a boozer, and his mother suffered from senile dementia. "About three years later my uncle's sister got a call from [the] sheriff's department informing her of an elderly woman who had the sister's address on a letter in her possession," Carpenter continued. The deputy who contacted Carpenter's

Picking cotton was hard work, but baling it was just plain dangerous. *Author's collection.*

West Texans took pride in posing next to the season's first bale of cotton, but one time a bale held a grisly surprise. *Author's collection.*

relative asked her if she had any missing relatives. The sister described her mother, and the officer said it sounded like the woman they had in protective custody. The elderly woman had been found wandering in the yard of a rent house and someone had called the sheriff, the deputy explained. Investigators looking into the matter learned that the house had been rented by a man who had his mother living with him, but no one knew where he had gone.

Finally, a deputy found a witness who recalled having seen the man walking in the direction of the cotton gin when it was ginning. Checking there, the deputy learned from the operator that he had given the man a job oiling the bearings above the point where the cotton was pushed into the large blades that stripped away the burrs and seeds. "The man had not been seen again and the operator figured that he had quit," Carpenter says.

Later, when the bales produced that fall were being moved around, someone noticed a dark stain on one of them. "It was blood," Carpenter goes on, "so they checked some other bales and found more blood, seven bales in all." The gin operator called the sheriff's office to report the grisly discovery. No trace of the missing man's body could be found, but the officers concluded that the man, likely drunk, had fallen into the machinery. Pieces of his body had ended up in multiple bales of cotton. The gin burned the stained bales, a practical if inelegant funeral pyre for a man who paid a hard price for his addiction. At least that's the story. Whether the man actually tumbled into a swirling maw of sharp blades and got baled or merely disappeared into the mist of alcoholism, this and the other body-in-a-bale story sound like a rural variation of the old body-in-a-large-dam legend.

The best example of this folklore category is the persistent legend that several construction workers fell into the concrete when the Hoover Dam was being built back during the 1930s in Nevada. Unable to rescue the unfortunate souls, the story goes, their still-healthy colleagues just kept pouring more concrete on them.

While the Hoover Dam tale has been quite credibly debunked (for one thing, engineers say a body could not be left to decompose in concrete because that would weaken the structure), similar stories are told of the Grand Coulee Dam on Washington's Columbia River. The body-in-the-concrete legend also has been associated with Lake Travis's Mansfield Dam in central Texas, and doubtless there are other dams with reputed construction worker burials.

One thing is indisputable: working in a cotton gin or at a major construction site has a few more risks associated with it than sitting in an office.

What Makes Texas...Texas

PECAN GAMES

Pecans are for pies and pralines and, for the more healthy minded, inclusion in salads or entrées. But there's more to the nut produced by Texas's official state tree than food value. At least there used to be. Early day Texas kids, not having a very wide variety of what used to be called "store-bought" toys, found ways to play with pecans before eating them.

Bill Ellis, born in 1919, grew up in Brownwood in the 1920s and '30s. As he recalled in his 2006 self-published memoir, *Rubber Guns: 'Bout a Little Texas Boy in a Texas '20s Town*, Brown County "is big pecan country." In fact, he wrote, for years the U.S. Department of Agriculture operated a pecan experiment station there. And in his youth just about every yard had a pecan tree or two.

When pecans began to come down from the branches in the fall, Ellis and his friends had a couple of games they played with them. The kids called the first game "Crackers." As Ellis wrote: "By trial and error I selected the hardest shell pecan that I could find, (usually a big native) and marked it with my name. I then approached a buddy with the challenge 'Crackers.' He would give me his hard shell pecan, and I would put the two side by side in my hands, and press them together." Whichever pecan broke under the pressure belonged to the loser, he said.

Naturally, some kids tried to "game" the game and resorted to sneaky means to develop a tougher pecan. Ellis said some players soaked their biggest hardshell in oil to make it even tougher, though he wrote that he doubted that really worked. Other kids got more elaborate in their cheating, drilling a small hole in the pecan, burning out the meat of the nut with a hot wire and then filling the cavity with hot lead. Ellis said boys with lead-filled "Crackers" would never let the opposing player hold his, a sure tell that someone was a cheater. But this heavy metal scam, the loaded dice of "Crackers," seems a bit fanciful since molten lead would have to be at least 621.43 degrees. Of course, if the pecan cavity had water in it the scheme might work, but like the warning goes, best not to try this at home. Besides, it's now known that lead is unhealthful.

The second game Ellis remembered playing with pecans was called "Hully-Gully." To let him tell it: "I would put from…three to eight pecans in my hands, shake them near the ear of a buddy's, and say, 'hully-gully.' He would guess the number of pecans. He had to then give me pecans equal to the number that his guess had missed, and then he got to 'hully-gully.' If he guessed right, he got all my pecans." Hully-gully is also a game kids used to play with marbles. Pecans are a logical and free substitute for store-bought marbles.

An experienced "hully-gully" player could employ several strategies to win. A saavy competitor might bend a couple of his fingers around some of the pecans he held so they couldn't make any noise when the shaking occurred. Or a player could shake very hard or hardly at all. Finally, a less-than-scrupulously-honest "hully-gully" guy could stuff so many pecans in his hands that they couldn't rattle.

Not mentioned in Ellis's book is the fact that pecans also used to be transformed into doll heads. All it took was a little paint to turn a pecan into a face that could be attached to a cotton-stuffed cloth body. Once an easy-to-make girls' toy, pecan dolls today are considered collectible folk art.

Over the years, industrious Texans doubtless have come up with other imaginative uses for pecans, but their highest and best purpose is their food value, especially when candied with baked yams for a Thanksgiving side dish.

Coffee in Merkel

When the visiting homeboy and his friend from the big city walked into Merkel's only drugstore for a cup of coffee that morning, none of the other coffee drinkers paid any attention whatsover. No "hiddy's," just a few casual looks. Conversation proceeded intermittently, borne of long acquaintance

Standing drugstore coffee break is a daily ritual in Merkel and elsewhere in West Texas. *Courtesy of Roger T. Moore.*

coupled with a rural tendency not to waste words. And all according to long-established if unwritten "rules."

Every day except Wednesdays, when the Merkel Drug Store is closed, local farmers and businessmen in this small Taylor County community gather for morning coffee. The coffee-drinking goes on no matter what, though individual circumstance does cause attendance to vary from day to day.

On this chilly morning, the first topic of conversation is the weather. Preceded by a good rain, a cold front had blown in a couple of days earlier. "Got down to thirty-one at my place," says one gimme-capped farmer. "Had ice on my windshields this morning."

"How much rain d'you get?" another asked.

"About three-quarters of an inch. Started in Friday evening and rained more Saturday."

One of the daily attendees is advertising executive and cartoonist Roger Moore, who grew up in Merkel. After living and working many years in Austin, he semi-retired and moved back to his old family farm in 2008. He says locals have been meeting for coffee every day for as long as he can remember.

"When I was little, the men collected at the feed store," Moore recalls. "My daddy would say, 'I'm gonna go pack a sack,' which meant he was going to the feed store for the free coffee they provided." Back then the men enjoyed their cup of Joe sitting on stacks of feed sacks, packing down the sacks. Later, the daily coffee club moved to the drugstore soda fountain. Even so, some of the men, including Moore's father, hated going from free to five-cent coffee.

The coffee ritual is not unique to Merkel. Since practically forever, Texans all across the state have practiced this little-known daily routine of coffee and conversation. Though more common in small towns, no-dues, no-officers coffee clubs occasionally develop in the bigger cities. Often, the metropolitan sippers grew up in small towns and carried their tradition with them.

"Daddy said coffee's the fount of all knowledge," Moore continues. "Sometimes rather than saying he was going to 'pack a sack,' he'd grab his hat and tell us he was 'going to school.'" Years later, sitting around drinking coffee is how Moore found out that the only way to keep rats out of the old pickup he keeps in his barn is to leave the hood up when he's not using it. "Rats like cover," he learned.

The daily coffee drinking looks to be a casual event, but according to Moore, practitioners adhere to strict if un-codified rules. "You don't introduce anybody," Moore begins. "Well, maybe if you sit right down next to somebody, the person you're with will say, 'This is ole so-and-so from wherever.' But the locals all know each other."

That brings up another rule: You don't acknowledge when people arrive. Or when they leave, for that matter. Interrupting someone is the most serious breach of coffee drinking etiquette, Moore says. Breaking in on another's conversation is hardly necessary in the first place. The pace of talk is seldom hurried enough to even tempt cutting someone off.

At the Merkel Drug these days, coffee is self-serve. What Moore's dad used to pay five cents for now costs ten times that, still a bargain compared with the urban café latte salons that charge the better part of a five-dollar bill for a cup. These other tongue-in-cheek prices are posted on the wall:

Small 54 cents
Medium 81 cents
Large $1.62

Refills, of course, are free.

Periodically, there being no waitress, someone will pick up the coffeepot and make the rounds, topping off everyone's cup.

"Saw your picture in the paper yesterday," one of the farmers ventured, looking at a ruddy-faced buddy peering out from under a John Deer hat.

The man looked puzzled. "I wasn't in the paper," he said.

"Yes you were…in the Farm Expo section," his friend said. "Your wife and kids sure looked pretty." (The joking inference being that he didn't.)

"Well, I can't afford to take the paper," he said.

"The picture said you were working on your farm," his friend continued. "Must have been fake."

While it might seem like these men are just starting their day, most coffee clubs convene after the early rising members have already done some work.

Discussing what ended up as a pretty good year for cotton, one of the "members" noted for the record that not every year is good when your crop depends on how much it rains and when. "I remember your daddy always used to say that if he had it to do over again, he'd build his house closer to town so he wouldn't have to drive past his fields every day," one of the farmers told Moore. "Too depressing in a bad year."

Politics, of course, is another staple of conversation. "He gives a good speech, but he don't say anything," one of the older men said of one candidate.

By 9:00 a.m., the soda fountain is as empty as a politician's promise. Until it's time for an afternoon cup.

Horse Troughs

Water troughs, better known in Texas as horse troughs, are intended for the hydration of livestock. But West Texas ranchers and their families have found far more use for these open containers of water than merely affording Old Dobbin a place to drink.

Horse troughs also played a role in many a Hollywood western as a handy receptacle for bad guys in saloon brawls. Nothing like knocking a drunken cowpoke in a slimy horse trough to put him in his place, so to speak. In the 1963 Paul Newman classic *Hud*, the coldhearted, hotblooded character played by the late actor while in his salad days seemed to think the ranch's horse trough could sober him up if he splashed his face enough.

In real life, many a ranch kid ran to the trough to stick an injured or burned limb in. Cartoon characters like Daffy Duck also found that a convenient horse trough could cure the effects of a shotgun blast or a hotfoot.

While the trough shown in *Hud* was a circular galvanized metal affair, first-generation Texas troughs were made of wood. Later, ranchers made concrete tanks and eventually turned to the galvanized tank. "They lined the inside of the wooden troughs with pitch," Merkel resident Roger Moore

Um.. could I get a BOTTLED water???

Horse troughs have many uses. *Cartoon by Roger T. Moore.*

recalls. "They always leaked a little, but not enough to make a difference." Despite the pitch, the troughs eventually sprouted some form of vegetation. Wet wood made a nice growth medium for algae, and the constant water supply encouraged other plants as well.

But in a country where water was and is always at a premium, a full horse trough was as good as a creek or river if neither body of water lay particularly close.

Moore remembers a wooden trough on his grandfather's place that the old man claimed had been the site of the first baptizing in that part of Taylor County. Other horse trough uses include:

- A place to obtain water for the radiator of your overheated Model T.
- A place to dunk someone who had offended you in some manner.
- A place to take an outdoor bath. Vaudaline R. Thomas, in her self-published book *Plum Creek Memorabilia*, recalled a West Texas cowboy who preferred bathing in the horse trough. One day when the wife of a neighbor drove up, she spotted the cowboy as he enjoyed his bath.

Every time he tried to get out, Thomas recalled, the lady revved the motor of her Model T to announce her continuing presence, forcing the hapless hand back into the water. "This went on for some 10 minutes," she wrote. "She was determined that he have one good Saturday bath."

- Horse troughs made a reservoir for minnows in anticipation of the next fishing trip. They ate mosquitoes, too.
- You could even keep a creek-caught bass or mess of perch in the horse trough for a time. Moore remembers one friend who put goldfish in his family's trough.
- On a hot day, dipping your hat in the trough provided a little natural air conditioning for a while.
- As long as a careful guard was kept, a horse trough made a great place to cool a watermelon.
- Throw in a block of ice and a horse trough made an excellent beer and soft drink cooler.
- In lake-shy West Texas, a horse trough could be as big as an ocean for a kid with a homemade toy boat.
- Finally, troughs attracted wildlife, from quail to deer.

Recollections

HOTBLOODED OVER ICE

With grim determination, a normally peaceful, law-abiding man who's just learned he's been done wrong starts to strap on his six-shooter aiming to make things right. Enter his pleading wife, who with tears, threats or both prevails on her husband to put the gun away and turn the figurative other cheek.

It's a cliché western movie scene, but in my family, one time it really happened. The injustice that nearly triggered an episode of Old West–style violence did not stem from the need to avenge a killing, deal with a philanderer or handle a horse thief. On a hot summer afternoon in the early 1900s, it had to do with ice.

The protagonist in this real-life western episode was my great-grandfather Adolph Wilke, a first-generation Texan whose father had come to Fredericksburg from Germany. It happened in Ballinger, then a bustling West Texas town on the upper Colorado River.

As my granddad, L.A. Wilke (1897–1984), told the story, his father for a time made his living operating an ice wagon. He got his sawdust-packed ice wholesale via train from Austin or San Antonio. After loading the standard 40-pound slabs into his wagon, he cut them down into 12.5-pound or 25-pound blocks and made his rounds selling them for five or ten cents a block.

Though frozen and often cloudy with ammonia that stunk when it melted, ice was a sure seller back then because electric refrigerators were not yet available. In fact, the first self-contained electric refrigerator did not hit the market in the United States until 1923. Great-granddad's customers placed a block of ice into wooden iceboxes that had pans beneath them to collect the water as the ice slowly melted. Ice deliveries usually were daily.

While he peddled a popular product, Granddad's father did not enjoy a monopoly. Another man, my granddad recalled his last name was Haley, also sold ice in Ballinger. One day, the competitor pulled his team up outside the depot and picked up a shipment of ice intended for Great-granddad and started selling it. On learning of this, as my granddad later put it, "Papa put on his gun (a .38 revolver) and was going to go to town" to discuss the matter with the other iceman.

At that point, my great-grandmother Mattie interceded and kept her justly furious husband from settling the theft issue in the manner of the late frontier. Granddad did not go into detail as to how his mother stopped his father from leaving their house with his gun, but he said her action likely averted a killing.

Adolph and Mattie Wilke in the 1920s. Mattie kept her husband from strapping on his six-shooter when he got hotheaded over stolen ice. *Author's collection.*

In the end, neither my great-granddad nor his business rival prevailed in the market. As Ballinger continued to grow and the technology got cheaper, someone finally opened an ice plant there and established their own delivery service.

Handy with a gun since his earlier days as a cowboy, Great-granddad got a job as a Runnels County sheriff's deputy. He ran the jail, which is where he lived with his family.

Thirty-six miles down the railroad tracks from Ballinger was San Angelo, where my future grandmother, Viola Helen Anderson, lived with her family. She remembered the excitement that came when the first ice factory opened in San Angelo. Her father would carry ice home with tongs. Their first icebox was just that, she said, a box with sawdust in it. Later, they got a commercial wooden icebox. "I thought we were the richest people in the world when we got our first real icebox," she later recalled.

Ice distributors printed cards for people to display outside their homes so deliverymen would know how much ice the family needed. They would carry the ice on their back and take it straight to the icebox. "You better have everything out of the way when they came in," she said.

She and Granddad got married in 1916. They did not get their first electric refrigerator until the mid-1920s, when they lived in Fort Worth. Even then, she hadn't wanted one, she said. She was satisfied with the old icebox method.

Talking about it years later, Granddad interjected that he had somehow tricked her into finally getting the newfangled applicance. "You were tricked a few times yourself," Grandmother countered.

Grandmother remembered one funny incident indirectly concerning ice. In May 1910, when she was twelve, the family living next door came down with smallpox. A yellow flag fluttered from their porch, signifying that the house had been quarantined.

Another neighbor was a widow whose son worked for the local daily, the *Standard*. One day the young man came running home from the newspaper office to announce the world was coming to an end, apparently because of the approach of Haley's comet. The widow rushed over to Grandmother's house to tell her mother of the impending disaster. The woman was very frightened, but my great-grandmother scoffed at the report. "Well," she finally said, "if the world's coming to an end, we might as well make some ice cream."

She told my grandmother to start breaking up some ice and then cranked up the central telephone exchange for a connection to the people next door

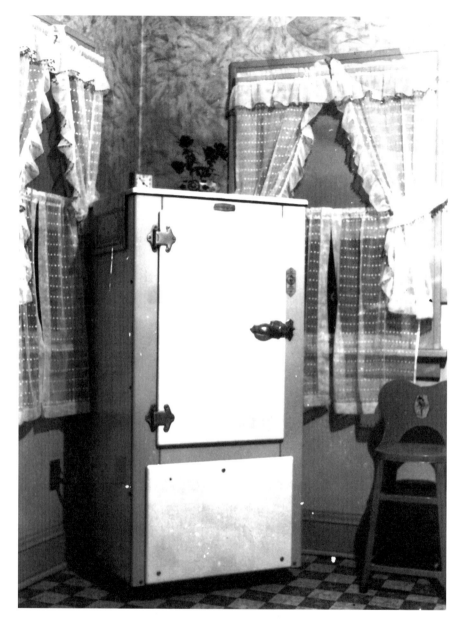

L.A. Wilke and his wife were so proud when they got their first electric refrigerator in the mid-1920s that he took a photograph of it. *Author's collection.*

with the smallpox. The end time at hand, she said, they might as well forget about the danger of contagion and come over for some ice cream before they died. That scared the fretful widow even more, grandmother said.

Of course, the people with smallpox stayed put and Haley's comet continued its interplanetary journey, leaving Earth no worse for the wear. But the Andersons and their nervous neighbors sure enjoyed their ice cream.

LOADING AMMO FOR BUFFALO BILL

Not everyone connected with Buffalo Bill Cody's Wild West Show got star billing. When the gray-bearded old scout's famous traveling performance came to Ballinger in 1910, my granddad (L.A. Wilke) played a role both important and minor—he helped reload the rifle ammunition so copiously expended during the show.

Years later, around 1975, Granddad recalled: "Not many men living today knew Buffalo Bill Cody, who helped to tame the West and then brought his feats to many people of the day, who admired his shooting skill with a Winchester rifle. It was my privilege not only to know him, but to reload his rifle cartridges with black powder and hand-cut cardboard wads for two years."

Another Texan who got to meet Buffalo Bill when his show came to the Lone Star State, Smith Moore, described Cody in his 1974 self-published book *Tall Tales*: "Colonel Cody was an erect, sinewy, active man in those days, with a white goatee, a large mustache, and white hair which hung down near his shoulders. He was a little taller than average…He had fiery blue eyes that could burn a hole through you."

After playing to a packed crowd in New York's Madison Square Garden on May 14, 1910—the venue of his first big show more than twenty years earlier—Cody announced that he was beginning his final tour. (Which turned out not to be true, but that's showbiz after all.) That fall, the Wild West Show came to Texas and worked its way around the state.

On November 10, 1910, the show's ninety-two railroad cars rolled into Dallas, arriving in four waves. The cars carried five hundred horses and 1,270 people ranging from the tent gang to the performers to Buffalo Bill himself. Wagons hauled the show's equipment and personnel from the depot to the show site, a field just to the southwest of the intersection of Commerce and Exposition Boulevard in what is now central Dallas. The show's press agent sent a notice to the *Dallas Morning News* and the rival *Times-Herald* that "there will be no street parade, for the reason that the parade fatigues the horses and performers."

Buffalo Bill's promotional team pasted posters like this all over town to hype his Wild West extravagaza. *Library of Congress.*

Evidently well rested, Buffalo Bill's congress of cowboys and Indians put on a good show. "Cowboy life was faithfully portrayed," the *News* reported, "and the other features of the show were as truthfully outlined."

After more than sixty-five years, Granddad could not remember just when Buffalo Bill and his entourage hit Ballinger that year, but he never forgot the experience. "Because at twelve years of age I was considered too young and too lightweight to drive tent stakes or to carry water I got the job of reloading blank cartridges," Granddad wrote. "My pay was a ticket to the show!"

Granddad told whoever did the local hiring that he had experience in loading Robin Hood shotgun shells and, by virtue of that, landed the reloading job. This was long before the government worried much about child labor or workplace safety, of course.

Though the youngster's only experience in recycling ammunition (not that the word "recycling" had its present usage back then) involved shotgun shells, the show needed brass rifle cartridges reloaded. "The hulls had been emptied in shooting exhibitions at his last show before coming to my hometown," Granddad continued. "I was too young to wonder if he had an extra supply on hand. I knew only that here a great shooter was honoring me with a ticket to see his exhibition for services rendered." Granddad told me that in addition to a pass to the show, he got to shake the affable colonel's hand. Cody also complimented him on his work.

Still sitting tall in the saddle, Cody choreographed his shows and put on a performance of his own. "Though Col. Cody has grown older, he bears well the burden of his years, and in appearance and action is about the same man who was the hero of boyhood days," the Dallas newspaper observed.

Staying in present tense, the newspaper went on to describe how the famous showman expended some of the shells my granddad soon would be reloading for him: "Mounted on his famous gray cow pony, the veteran plainsman gives an extraordinary exhibition of marksmanship which denotes he has also retained the keen eyesight that at one time made him a terror to Indian marauders and evil doers. Going at full speed he breaks glass balls tossed into the air in rapid succession, and very infrequently did his bullets fail to find and smash the target."

Sam Baker, another marksman in the show, doubtless emptied many of the cartridges my granddad reloaded. "In his exhibition of expert shooting," the *Morning News* continued, "[Baker] displayed extraordinary skill. Holding his weapon in various and uncommon positions he broke in succession a score or more of targets without a single miss."

THE OCTOBER BARREL

Eight-year-old Viola Helen Anderson did not grasp that the U.S. stood on the brink of a financial crisis that would come to be called the Panic of 1906. All the San Angelo girl cared about was that her daddy had died.

On a cold, rainy day that winter, a big load of merchandise arrived at the March Brothers General Store on Beauregard, the West Texas town's main thoroughfare. That's where Helen's father worked, and no matter the weather, he insisted on supervising the wagon's unloading. Richard Anderson took a cold that developed into pneumonia. Back then, doctors called it the galloping consumption. He died on January 16, and they buried him in Fairmount Cemetery.

"He was a kind and gentle man and we really depended on him," Helen remembered a lifetime later, "but Mama and I had to keep going, and we did."

While Helen attended school, Minta Gafford Anderson supported them in the midst of a growing national money shortage by sewing and taking in boarders.

Viola Helen Anderson about the time her father died. *Author's collection.*

Across the state, Lizzie Gafford Kincaid and her husband Jim—Helen's aunt and uncle—struggled to keep their dry goods store open in the little town of Lindale, north of Tyler. They sold everything from candy to coffins. "Mama and Aunt Lizzie were very close," Helen said, "but Mama didn't have much use for Uncle Jim, who fought for the Union in the Civil War. Mama's family's farm in Mississippi had been burned by Yankees and more than forty years hadn't dulled her memory."

When school let out for the summer, the new widow and her daughter packed their big trunk and took the train to East Texas. While her mother spent time with her sister, visiting, sewing and helping with the canning, Helen made friends with the daughter of the man who owned the hotel adjacent to the railroad. Behind the hotel, Helen and the other little girl laid rocks on the ground to make the outline of an imaginary house. Finding scattered pieces of broken china, they used those to set an imaginary table. "A train coming in would mean a meal was about to be served at the hotel, so we'd scoot in and collect all the food we wanted from my friend's mother," she recalled. When her friend could not play, Helen spent time in her family's store playing solo hide-and-go-seek and freely helping herself to the candy bins.

They stayed in Lindale most of the summer, finally making the long train ride back to San Angelo in time for the start of school. Back in West Texas,

The Andersons lived in this frame house on the northern edge of San Angelo. *Author's collection.*

Helen missed her friend and their simple playhouse, her aunt and uncle and the candy in their store.

One day in October, Helen happened to take her time coming home from school. She only hurried when she walked through the old cemetery, where they had been digging up graves to make room for a new high school. Jumping over the open graves, she tried not to notice the coffin handles and shoe heels in the piles of dirt.

"Mama was a little put out with me when I finally got home," she recalled. Then Helen noticed a large wooden barrel in the middle of their small kitchen. She assumed it held sugar. "Mama made a lot of preserves, but I couldn't understand why she would need a whole barrel of sugar," she said. "Mama pried the boards off the top and I scrambled up on a chair to look inside. All I saw was peanuts." The arrival of a barrel of peanuts seemed even more incomprehensible. Her mother could barely afford the basics, certainly not a luxury like goobers.

"I was still puzzling over it when she fished inside and pulled out an apron," Helen said. "Her next thrust produced a sack she handed to me. It was my favorite candy. Mama told me to help her, and my first dip brought out a comb and brush Mama said I could have."

Finally, Helen understood. Uncle Jim and Aunt Lizzie had sent them a treasure chest in a fifty-five-gallon barrel. It held assorted notions and knickknacks, clothing, buttons, lace, powder jars, writing tablets for school, pencils, dime novels, fruit, preserves, sweet potatoes, ribbon cane and persimmons—a veritable general store packed in peanuts.

"Every October we got our barrel from Uncle Jim and Aunt Lizzie," Helen recalled. "Mama never had much money, but the October Barrel wasn't charity. It was just understood back then that people had to help people. I don't know how many times Mama got called out in the middle of the night when someone was sick, dead or having a baby."

Of course, Minta did things for her sister, too. She even sewed for her Yankee brother-in-law.

The last October Barrel came in 1916. "By that time," Helen said, "I was married and pretty soon after that barrel came, my husband got a job with a newspaper in Fort Worth and we moved. Not long after that, Uncle Jim and Aunt Lizzie sold their store and came back to the San Angelo area."

Helen never understood why her aunt and uncle chose to ship the barrel in October instead of before Christmas, but she knew how much it meant to a widow and a fatherless girl.

For the rest of her long life, especially when the days got shorter and the weather turned cooler, my grandmother remembered the October Barrel and what it taught her.

About the Author

M ike Cox, an elected member of the Texas Institute of Letters, is the author of nineteen nonfiction books. After nearly two decades as an award-winning journalist, he began a long career as a state employee, first as a spokesman for the Texas Department of Public Safety, then as communication manager for the Texas Department of Transportation and currently, following a short-lived retirement, as a spokesman for the Texas Parks and Wildlife Department. He and his wife, Linda, and daughter, Hallie, live in Austin, but he visits West Texas as often as he can.

Visit us at
www.historypress.net